WORKBOOK / LABORATORY MANUAL FOR

Foundation Course in Spanish

SIXTH EDITION

LAUREL H. TURK • DePauw University

AURELIO M. ESPINOSA, Jr. • Stanford University

CARLOS A. SOLÉ, Jr. • University of Texas, Austin

D. C. HEATH AND COMPANY

Lexington, Massachusetts • Toronto

International Standard Book Number: 0-669-06996-5

Preface

The *Workbook/Laboratory Manual* has been prepared to supplement *Foundation Course in Spanish, Sixth Edition*. It is designed to assist in the development of the student's command of the grammatical, phonological, and lexical elements of the Text. In addition, the supplement is a useful instrument to help the instructor and the student verify the degree to which material has been learned and understood. These objectives are best achieved if the exercises in the *Workbook* are completed *after* the corresponding material has been covered and mastered in class, as well as in the language laboratory.

In the *Workbook*, the emphasis is on step-by-step learning based on exercises that are graded in difficulty. The material covers a spectrum of activities from simple dictation and a wide variety of grammar drills to questions requiring a written response and English-to-Spanish translation. Exercises on pronunciation are included for Lessons 1–12. Many changes have been made in the exercises of this edition of the *Workbook*, principally to conform with changes made in the Sixth Edition of *Foundation Course in Spanish*.

The *Laboratory Manual* is to be used in conjunction with the tapes indicated at the beginning of each lesson. The exercises are of three kinds: exercises on the dialogues, in which comprehension and vocabulary are stressed; pronunciation and intonation drills; and exercises involving structure, listening, and writing, in which a combination of skills is required.

The dialogue exercises are presented in three forms: multiple-choice questions; sentence-completion exercises; and true/false exercises. In all cases a written response is required. For the pronunciation drills (for Lessons 1–14), the student not only repeats sounds and phrases pronounced by the speaker, but also practices sound discrimination. The exercises on intonation (for Lessons 15–22) supplement the section on intonation contained in the Text, Appendix A; they cover the basic principles of Spanish intonation. The structure, listening, and writing sections include activities of various kinds: exercises on important grammatical points; transformation drills involving verb forms and subject and object pronouns; English-to-Spanish translation; and dictation exercises. In most cases, the student's responses are verified by the speaker; in the remaining cases, they are to be checked by the instructor.

Keys to the exercises in this *Workbook/Laboratory Manual* appear on pages T45 through T65 of the Annotated Edition of the Text.

Abbreviations used are:

f.	feminine	*indir.*	indirect	*p(p).*	page(s)
fam.	familiar	*m.*	masculine	*pl.*	plural
imp.	imperfect	*obj.*	object	*sing.*	singular

Laurel H. Turk
Aurelio M. Espinosa, Jr.
Carlos A. Solé, Jr.

Contents

Workbook

Lección 1

I. Dictation

The teacher will read two or three exchanges from the dialogues.

....

....

....

....

Compare what you have written with your Text, p. 14.

II. Pronunciation exercises

A. Review the sounds of Spanish **c** (and **z**), **qu,** and **k** (Text, p. 15); then circle each letter or group of letters that is pronounced like English *c* in *cat:*

aquí	clase	ejercicio	lección
necesito	practicar	pronuncia	¿qué?

B. Review linking (Text, p. 9); then rewrite the following sentences, each of which may be considered one breath group, dividing them into syllables and underlining the stressed syllables, following the model. Note that the forms of the definite article (**el**) are not pronounced as stressed words in Spanish.

MODEL: ¿Habla usted alemán?   *¿Ha-bla͜ us-te-d͜ a-le-mán?*

1. ¿Qué lenguas estudias? ....

2. ¿Preparas el ejercicio? ....

3. No hablamos inglés.   ....

III. Supply the corresponding subject pronouns when necessary:

1. .... estudiamos español.

2. .... estudio inglés y .... (*m.*) estudia alemán.

3. .... (*emphatic*) hablo italiano con la familia.

4. .... (*formal*) habla francés en casa.

5. .... (*f. sing.*) y yo necesitamos estudiar más.

6. .... preparo los ejercicios en el laboratorio.

7. .... *(formal)* no estudian mucho.

8. .... *(formal sing.)* y .... *(m. sing.)* no preparan los ejercicios.

9. .... pronuncias bien y .... *(f. sing.)* pronuncia mal.

10. .... *(emphatic)* no hablamos alemán.

IV. Forms and uses of the definite article

A. Write the corresponding definite article:

.... clase   .... francés   .... tarde

.... español   .... alumnas   .... profesores

.... día   .... expresión   .... familias

.... palabra   .... lecciones   .... conversación

B. Supply the definite article when necessary:

1. No hablamos .... inglés con .... profesora.

2. Ella pronuncia muy bien .... francés y .... español.

3. .... profesor habla con .... alumnos.

4. Nosotros preparamos .... lecciones en .... casa.

5. Usted habla .... italiano y ella habla .... español.

6. Ellos practican .... ejercicios en .... clase.

V. Negative and interrogative sentences

A. Write in the negative:

1. Preparamos los ejercicios en clase. ....

....

2. Mario pronuncia bien el español. ....

....

3. Luisa necesita practicar más. ....

....

4. Ella practica en casa. ....

....

B. Write negative answers, following the model.

MODEL: ¿Habla ella inglés?   *No, señor (señora, señorita), ella no habla inglés.*

1. ¿Practican ustedes mucho el español?

....

2. ¿Estudia él todos los días?

....

3. ¿Pronuncia ella bien?

....

4. ¿Hablamos nosotros inglés en clase?

....

C. Change to questions:

1. El alumno estudia español. ....

2. Mario pronuncia bien. ....

3. Ustedes hablan italiano. ....

4. Ellas practican la lección. ....

VI. Write in Spanish, using formal forms for "you":

1. Good afternoon, Mario. What language are you studying? ....

....

2. I am studying Spanish now. ....

....

3. Do you prepare the lessons every day? ....

....

4. Yes, ma'am, and I practice the language a lot with Louise. ....

....

5. Do the students prepare the exercises at home? ....

....

6. We prepare the pronunciation exercises in the laboratory. ....

....

7. Louise already pronounces Spanish quite well. ....

....

8. The Spanish teacher (*f.*) speaks Spanish and French. ....

....

VII. Write answers to these questions, using complete sentences:

1. ¿Qué lengua estudiamos en la clase de español?

....

2. ¿Hablamos inglés en clase?

....

3. ¿Qué lengua habla usted en casa?

....

4. ¿Pronuncia usted bien el español?

....

5. ¿Estudia usted mucho todos los días?

....

6. ¿Qué ejercicios preparan los alumnos en el laboratorio?

....

....

Lección 2

I. Dictation

The teacher will read two or three exchanges from the dialogues.

....

....

....

....

Compare what you have written with your Text, p. 26.

II. Pronunciation exercises

A. Review the sounds of Spanish **d** (Text, p. 28); then circle each **d** that is pronounced like a weak English *th* in *this:*

cuadro	estudiar	grande	pared
un día	dos días	¿dónde?	con dos

B. Rewrite the two sentences of the setting of the first dialogue of this lesson, dividing them into breath groups (by means of a vertical line); then divide the breath groups of the second sentence into syllables and underline the stressed syllables. Note that prepositions (**en**) and forms of the definite article (**los**) are not pronounced as stressed words in Spanish:

....

....

....

....

III. Forms and uses of the definite and indefinite articles and of adjectives

A. Supply the corresponding indefinite article when necessary:

1. Yo soy .... alumno y usted es .... profesor.

2. Luisa es .... cubana; no es .... mexicana.

3. Hay .... cuaderno y .... lápiz en la mesa.

4. En la pared hay .... pizarra y .... mapas.

5

5. .... estudiantes (*f.*) llegan ahora.

6. La muchacha que tiene .... libro es .... chilena.

B. Write in the plural:

1. El cuadro es bonito. ....

2. La pared es blanca. ....

3. El lápiz es negro. ....

4. La alumna es mexicana. ....

5. La casa es muy bonita. ....

6. ¿Es bueno el profesor? ....

C. Complete with the corresponding form of the adjective:

1. (amarillo)   ¿Son .... las mesas?

2. (rojo)   ¿Son .... los libros?

3. (francés)   ¿Es .... la alumna?

4. (mexicano)   ¿Es .... el profesor?

5. (chileno)   Nosotros no somos ....

6. (inglés)   Los muchachos son ....

7. (azul)   Las paredes son ....

8. (negro)   La pizarra es ....

IV. Complete with the corresponding form of the present indicative tense of the verb:

(ser) 1. La familia de Ana .... de México. 2. Ana y Carlos ....

mexicanos. 3. Yo .... colombiano. 4. ¿................... tú español?

(tener) 5. ¿ .... usted un lápiz? 6. Sí, señora, yo .... un lápiz.

7. Nosotros también .... papel y unas plumas. 8. ¿Qué lección ....

ustedes que estudiar ahora?

V. Use of the relative pronoun *que*

Combine the two statements into one, following the model.

MODEL: Carlos tiene dos lápices. Los lápices son azules.
         Los lápices que Carlos tiene son azules.

1. Tenemos dos libros. Los libros son interesantes.

   ....

2. El estudiante es chileno. El estudiante tiene un cuaderno.

   ....

3. Tengo unos mapas. Son de México y de España.

   ....

4. Los alumnos tienen mesas. Las mesas son de color marrón.

   ....

VI. Form a sentence, making the necessary changes in the verb and supplying the definite article when required.

MODEL: rojo / ser / lápiz   *El lápiz es rojo.*

1. en casa / Mario y yo / ejercicios / preparar

   ....

2. carteles / Carlos / muchos / tener / de España

   ....

3. fotografías / son / del libro / interesantes

   ....

4. en la cafetería / comer / nosotros / todos los días

   ....

VII. Write in Spanish:

1. Charles and Anthony, who are students from South America, are talking in the cafeteria. ....

   ....

   ....

7

2. They eat there every day. ....

    ....

3. Charles is from Colombia; he is not (a) North American. ....

    ....

4. There are some (a few) students from Spain here also. ....

    ....

5. The students study hard and they already speak English well. ....

    ....

6. Where is Louise from? We think that she is English. ....

    ....

7. The teacher (*f.*) who is eating with a group of students is French. ....

    ....

8. The book that has the photographs in color is very attractive. ....

    ....

VIII. Write answers to these questions, using complete sentences:

1. ¿Es usted norteamericano (norteamericana)?

    ....

2. ¿Es de España el profesor (la profesora)?

    ....

3. ¿Qué hay en las paredes de la sala de clase?

    ....

4. ¿Tiene usted un libro o un cuaderno?

    ....

5. ¿Tienen ustedes que estudiar mucho?

    ....

6. ¿Come usted en casa o en la cafetería?

    ....

Lección 3

I. Dictation

The teacher will read two or three exchanges from the dialogues:

....

....

....

....

....

Compare what you have written with your Text, p. 40.

II. Pronunciation exercises

A. Review the sounds of Spanish **b** and **v** (Text, p. 41); then circle each **b** and **v** that is pronounced with the breath continuing to pass through a narrow opening between the lips:

bebemos	conversación	hablan	no vamos
es verdad	también	voy	viven

B. Rewrite the two sentences of the setting of the second dialogue, dividing them into breath groups and syllables, and underline the stressed syllables. Note that conjunctions (**y, mientras**) and prepositions (**de**) are not pronounced as stressed words in Spanish:

....

....

....

....

III. Complete with the corresponding form of the present indicative tense of the verb:

1. (tomar) Nosotros .... el desayuno a eso de las ocho.

2. (tomar) Laura .... el almuerzo a las doce y cuarto.

3. (cenar) Yo .... más o menos a las seis.

4. (ser) Tres de los estudiantes .... españoles.

9

5. (ser) .... la una de la mañana.

6. (ser) Ya .... las dos de la tarde.

7. (beber) Laura y Jorge .... un refresco.

8. (mirar) Ellos .... las fotografías.

9. (vivir) Carolina no .... cerca de la residencia.

10. (vivir) Laura y yo .... lejos de aquí.

11. (vivir) Tú .... en casa, ¿verdad?

12. (escribir) Ellos .... las cartas en la biblioteca.

13. (ir) ¿A qué hora .... tú a la clase de español?

14. (ir) Yo .... a la universidad por la tarde.

15. (ir) ¿Adónde .... ustedes tan temprano?

16. (tener) Yo .... una clase a las ocho.

IV. Telling time

Write in Spanish:

1. At 5:00 P.M. ....

2. At 9:10 A.M. ....

3. At 3:45 P.M. ....

4. At about 11:00 P.M. ....

5. It's 1:15. ....

6. It's 4:25. ....

7. It's 7:30. ....

8. It's 10:40. ....

V. Form a sentence, making the necessary changes in the verb:

1. tomar el desayuno / en la cafetería / Jorge / casi siempre

....

2. veinte estudiantes / creo que / en la clase de español / hay

....

10

3. de la tarde / al laboratorio / yo ir / a las cuatro

   ....

4. temprano / ir / a la biblioteca / yo tener que

   ....

5. ¿no es verdad? / una carta / escribir / usted ir a

   ....

VI. Write the numerals in Spanish:

1. (17) .... mesas   6. (22) .... alumnos

2. (12) .... horas   7. (11) .... noches

3. (18) .... cartas   8. (19) .... plumas

4. (21) .... libros   9. (15) .... relojes

5. (21) .... sillas   10. (31) .... mapas

VII. Write in Spanish:

1. Ann and Caroline live in an apartment near the university. ....

   ....

2. It is almost 7:30 A.M., and Ann is writing a letter. ....

   ....

3. She has to go to the restaurant (in order) to take breakfast. ....

   ....

4. She has two classes in the morning and one in the afternoon. ....

   ....

5. She doesn't need an hour (in order) to arrive at the university. ....

   ....

6. George and Laura are talking about meal hours in the university residence halls. ....

   ....

7. They generally have breakfast at 7:30 A.M. ....

   ....

11

8. If they have classes in the afternoon, they have lunch at about 12:00. ....

   ....

9. In the residence hall where Laura lives, they have supper at 6:15 P.M. ....

   ....

10. The students study in the library until 10:30 P.M., more or less. ....

   ....

VIII. Write answers to these questions, using complete sentences:

1. ¿Vive usted en una residencia de la universidad?

   ....

2. ¿A qué hora toma usted el desayuno?

   ....

3. ¿Cuántas clases tiene usted por la mañana?

   ....

4. ¿A qué hora toma usted el almuerzo?

   ....

5. ¿Prepara usted la lección de español por la noche o por la tarde?

   ....

6. ¿A qué hora cena usted generalmente?

   ....

Lección 4

I. Dictation

The teacher will read two or three exchanges from the dialogues.

....

....

....

....

....

Compare what you have written with your Text, p. 54.

II. Pronunciation exercises

A. Rewrite the following sentences, each of which may be considered one breath group, dividing them into syllables and underlining the stressed syllables:

1. Es un grupo grande. ....

2. Miguel es argentino. ....

3. Jorge no es inglés. ....

B. Review the sounds of Spanish **g** (Text, p. 56); then circle each **g** or **gu** in the above sentences that is pronounced like a weak English *g* in *go*.

III. Verb forms and agreement

A. Rewrite the following sentences, using the new subjects:

1. Alberto recibe muchas cartas. (Alberto y yo)

....

2. Jorge viene a nuestra casa. (Mis amigos)

....

3. Yo no sé su dirección. (Nosotros)

....

4. Nosotros queremos leer el artículo. (Yo)

   ....

5. Mario va a comprar un diccionario. (Yo)

   ....

6. ¿Lees tú revistas españolas? (ustedes)

   ....

7. Mi compañero de cuarto necesita ir a la biblioteca. (Uds.)

   ....

8. ¿Aprenden ustedes las frases difíciles? (tú)

   ....

B. Complete with the corresponding form of the present indicative tense of the verb:

   1. (comprar) Jorge .... libros y yo .... revistas.

   2. (querer)   Yo .... cenar y ellos .... tomar un refresco.

   3. (escribir) Tú .... una carta y Miguel .... sus ejercicios.

   4. (ir)   Yo .... a las nueve y tú .... a la una.

   5. (saber)   Ellos .... que yo no .... su dirección.

   6. (leer)   Laura .... una carta mientras yo .... el periódico.

IV. Write affirmative answers to the following questions:

   1. ¿Olvida Ud. sus libros?   ....

   2. ¿Estudian Uds. sus lecciones?   ....

   3. ¿Vienes con tu amigo?   ....

   4. ¿Leen Uds. mis libros?   ....

   5. ¿Va Ud. con su hermana?   ....

   6. ¿Tienes tú mi lápiz?   ....

   7. ¿Sabe él mi dirección?   ....

   8. ¿Vives con tu familia?   ....

14

V. Position of adjectives

Rewrite, placing the adjectives in the correct position, following the model:

MODEL: mi / nuevo—reloj   *mi reloj nuevo*

1. mis / largas—cartas   ....

2. muchas / fáciles—frases   ....

3. las / españolas—elecciones   ....

4. varios / excelentes—mapas   ....

5. tres / cortos—artículos   ....

6. unas / pequeñas—sillas   ....

VI. Complete with the corresponding forms of the present indicative tense of *ser*:

1. La universidad no .... grande. 2. Los periódicos .... para Miguel. 3. No

.... difícil aprender las palabras. 4. ¿Qué hora ....? 5. .... las dos y

media. 6. La familia de Alberto .... de la Argentina. 7. Mi profesor de español no

.... peruano. 8. Yo .... norteamericano (norteamericana). 9. Tú ....

de México. 10. La pizarra .... negra. 11. ¿De quién .... el cuaderno?

12. ¿Para quiénes .... las cartas? 13. ¿................. yo estudiante? 14. No, Ud.

.... profesor.

VII. Write in Spanish, using affirmative and negative singular commands:

1. Study here; don't study in the library.

    ....

2. Eat now; don't eat a lot.

    ....

3. Write in Spanish; don't write in English.

    ....

VIII. Write in Spanish, using familiar singular forms for "you":

1. The city is quite large and it is also very old. ....

....

2. It has an excellent bookstore that receives many foreign books. ....

....

3. George and Michael want to buy a dictionary there; it is for Michael. ....

....

4. It is necessary to read a lot in order to learn new words and expressions. ....

....

5. Look, George, there are several Spanish magazines here. ....

....

6. The magazine has a short article on the elections in Spain. ....

....

7. The bookstore also has Spanish newspapers that come by airmail. ....

....

8. Send a Spanish newspaper to my address every week, please. ....

....

9. The boys want to read more news about the Hispanic world. ....

....

10. There aren't many news items about Spain in our television programs. ....

....

IX. Write answers to these questions, using complete sentences:

1. ¿Dónde compran los estudiantes los libros que necesitan?

....

2. ¿Quiere Ud. comprar un diccionario de la lengua española?

....

3. ¿Tienen libros extranjeros en la librería de la universidad?

....

16

4. ¿Recibe la librería periódicos españoles?

   ....

5. ¿Lee Ud. el periódico de la universidad?

   ....

6. ¿Hay noticias del mundo hispánico en el periódico de la universidad? ....

   ....

7. ¿Mira Ud. muchos programas de televisión? ....

   ....

8. ¿Mira Ud. los programas de televisión por la mañana o por la tarde? ....

   ....

Lección 5

I. Dictation

The teacher will read two or three exchanges from the dialogues.

....

....

....

....

....

Compare what you have written with your Text, p. 68.

II. Pronunciation exercises

A. Review the pronunciation of the diphthongs **ie** and **ei** (**ey**) (Text, p. 70); then rewrite the following words and phrases, dividing them into syllables and underlining the stressed syllables:

veintisiete   ....

las seis y diez   ....

¿quién viene?   ....

mi hermano   ....

sabe inglés   ....

B. Review the sounds of **r** and **rr** in Spanish (Text, p. 70); then circle each **r** and **rr** that is strongly trilled in Spanish:

ahora	hablar	marrón	pared	pizarra
refresco	regresar	rojo	tarde	un rato

III. Complete each sentence, writing the corresponding form of the present indicative tense of the conjugated verb:

1. Tu padre está trabajando todavía.

Yo   ....

Uds.   ....

Diana y yo ....

Tú ....

2. María no conoce la ciudad.

Uds. ....

Nosotros ....

Yo ....

Tú ....

IV. The personal a

Complete with the personal **a** when necessary:

1. ¿Quiere Ud. llamar .... sus padres? 2. Estamos mirando .... la televisión. 3. Buscamos .... la profesora. 4. Conozco bien .... Tomás. 5. ¿Conocen Uds. ....la ciudad donde vivo? 6. ¿Tiene Diana .... muchos amigos suramericanos? 7. No escribas (tú) .... la frase todavía. 8. Ellos no van a olvidar .... su amiga.

V. Review the uses of *ser* in Lesson 4; then complete with the corresponding form of the verb:

1. Diana y María .... hermanas. 2. ¿De quién .... el lápiz? 3. ¿De qué color .... las sillas? 4. ¿De qué país .... Ud.? 5. Tomás y yo .... amigos. 6. No .... fácil aprender las expresiones. 7. Yo no .... del Uruguay. 8. Las revistas .... para Alberto. 9. Ya .... las once y media de la noche. 10. La librería .... muy pequeña. 11. Jorge y yo no .... norteamericanos. 12. Ellos creen que tú .... español.

VI. Uses of *estar*

A. Complete with the corresponding form of **estar**:

1. ¿Cómo .... Uds.? 2. Nosotros .... muy cansados. 3. ¿Dónde .... tus hermanos? 4. Ellos .... en la biblioteca. 5. Mi hermana .... trabajando en Buenos Aires. 6. ¿................. tú descansando ahora? 7. No, yo .... escribiendo los ejercicios. 8. ¿Cómo .... tú? 9. Yo .... un poco enfermo. 10. Nosotros no .... muy ocupados.

20

B. Review the agreement of adjectives (Text, pp. 31–32); then complete each sentence:

1. Mi padre está enfermo hoy.

    Nosotras   ....

    Yo *(m.)*   ....

    Mis hermanos   ....

    Mi madre   ....

2. ¿Está ocupada la profesora?

    ¿.. tus hermanos?

    ¿.. Uds. *(f.)*?

    ¿.. tu padre?

    ¿.. tú *(f.)*?

VII. Supply the correct form of *estar* or *ser,* as required:

1. María, que .... trabajando en Buenos Aires, ... la hermana de Diana.

2. Ella .... aquí de visita; .... en la casa de sus padres. 3. Buenos Aires,

que .... la capital de la Argentina, ... una ciudad muy atractiva. 4. Los

padres de María no .... viejos; ellos .... muy contentos con la visita de su

hija. 5. .... las cinco de la tarde y el padre de María .... trabajando

todavía. 6. Él .... un poco cansado, ¿no .... verdad?

VIII. Uses of *conocer* and *saber*

Complete each sentence, using the corresponding form of the present indicative tense of **conocer** or **saber,** as required:

1. ¿.................... Uds. si Diana está en casa? 2. Yo no .... al señor Ortega.

3. Yo .... que ella está muy ocupada. 4. Ella no .... hablar francés.

5. ¿.................... Ud. a mis hermanos? 6. Ellos siempre .... las lecciones.

7. Nosotros no .... a tu profesor. 8. Yo .... el país muy bien.

IX. Write in Spanish, using the familiar forms for "you":

1. Diane and Thomas, who are classmates, are taking *(progressive)* a cold drink in the cafeteria.

   ....

   ....

2. Thomas is a South American student; he is studying *(progressive)* in the United States. ....

   ....

   ....

3. He is going to return soon to Montevideo, the capital of Uruguay. ....

   ....

4. Diane's sister is working in Buenos Aires, which is a very large city. ....

   ....

   ....

5. Diane is very happy because her sister arrives from Argentina today. ....

   ....

   ....

6. We don't know how long *(use* **cuánto tiempo***)* Mary is going to be here. ....

   ....

   ....

7. We believe that she is going to spend two weeks with her family. ....

   ....

   ....

8. Don't you want to meet Mary? Her plane arrives at five o'clock. ....

   ....

   ....

9. You know which (one) *(use* **cuál***)* is our house, don't you? ....

   ....

10. "Do you want to come at eight o'clock?" "Gladly. See you soon." ....

   ....

   ....

11. Mary arrives at her parents' house at about six o'clock; she is very tired. ....

....

....

12. The trip by plane is very long; she has to rest a while. ....

....

....

X. Write answers to these questions, using complete sentences:

1. ¿Está Ud. estudiando ahora?

....

2. ¿Está Ud. contento (contenta) con sus clases?

....

3. ¿Lee Ud. libros sobre el mundo hispánico?

....

4. ¿Cuál es la capital del Uruguay?

....

5. ¿Sabe Ud. si su profesor (profesora) recibe periódicos mexicanos?

....

6. ¿Quiere Ud. trabajar en un país extranjero?

....

Lectura 1

A. List the plural nouns in the *Lectura*, Text, pp. 84–85, in their singular forms (with the exception of **los informes, los Pirineos**), preceded by the corresponding definite article:

....

....

....

....

....

....

....

....

....

....

B. Circle the cognates:

1. España y Portugal ocupan la mayor parte de la Península Ibérica.

2. Madrid, la capital de España, está en el centro del país.

3. Es una ciudad moderna que tiene más de cuatro millones de habitantes.

4. Barcelona, que está en la costa del Mar Mediterráneo, es el puerto principal de España.

5. La influencia árabe es evidente en la agricultura, las industrias, la música y en otros aspectos de la vida andaluza.

6. En la producción de mercurio, de plomo y de uranio, España es una de las primeras naciones del mundo.

7. El turismo también tiene un lugar importante en la economía española.

8. En cuanto a la forma de gobierno, España es una monarquía constitucional.

9. La lengua oficial de España, el español, es una de las lenguas verdaderamente universales.

10. La contribución de los países americanos a la lengua común es especialmente importante.

11. Nuestras relaciones comerciales, políticas y culturales con los países de habla española tienen mucha importancia.

12. La influencia de España y de los países hispánicos en muchos aspectos de la cultura en general es considerable.

Lección 6

I. Dictation

The teacher will read two or three exchanges from the dialogues.

....

....

....

....

....

Compare what you have written with your Text, p. 90.

II. Pronunciation exercise

Review division of words into syllables, word stress, and breath groups (Text, pp. 6, 7, and 92); then rewrite the following sentences, dividing them into breath groups and syllables, and underlining the stressed syllables:

1. Mi hermana María está aquí de visita.

....

....

2. Rita y Enriqueta charlan de sus estudios.

....

....

III. Demonstrative adjectives

Rewrite the following sentences, making the demonstrative adjective and the noun plural, and making the necessary changes in agreement:

1. Voy a comprar este lápiz.

....

2. Quiero leer ese libro.

....

27

3. Vamos a estudiar en aquella ciudad.

....

4. Puedo ver aquel mapa.

....

5. Conocemos bien esa universidad.

....

6. Esta silla es nueva.

....

7. Ese programa es excelente.

....

8. Aquel estudiante es extranjero.

....

IV. Forms of irregular verbs

Write the verb forms in the present indicative tense which correspond to each subject:

	poder	*salir*	*traer*	*ver*
1. tú	....	....	....	....
2. Ud.	....	....	....	....
3. yo	....	....	....	....
4. él y yo	....	....	....	....
5. ellos	....	....	....	....

V. Direct object pronouns

A. Rewrite each sentence, substituting object pronouns for noun objects and modifiers:

1. Rita escribe la carta. ....

2. Leo el periódico. ....

3. Miramos el horario. ....

4. Ana abre las puertas. ....

5. ¿Buscas tú a Tomás? ....

6. ¿Esperan Uds. al profesor? ....

B. Write affirmative answers, substituting direct object pronouns for noun objects and modifiers, following the model.

MODEL: ¿Abre Jorge las ventanas?   *Sí, las abre.*

1. ¿Llama Ud. a Rita? ....

2. ¿Esperas a las chicas? ....

3. ¿Miras las fotografías? ....

4. ¿Traen Uds. los libros? ....

5. ¿Conocen Uds. a María? ....

6. ¿Ven Uds. el avión? ....

C. Write negative answers, substituting direct object pronouns for noun objects and modifiers, watching the position of the object pronoun:

MODEL: ¿Lees el periódico?   *No, no lo leo.*

1. ¿Ves a mis hermanos? ....

2. ¿Sabes la hora? ....

3. ¿Conoces a mi madre? ....

4. ¿Aprenden Uds. la frase? ....

5. ¿Reciben Uds. esta revista? ....

6. ¿Escuchan Uds. ese programa? ....

VI. Spanish verbs which take direct objects without the prepositions of their English equivalents

Write in Spanish (the personal **a,** of course, must not be omitted):

1. Henrietta is looking for an apartment. ....

....

2. Do you (*formal sing.*) listen to many radio programs? ....

....

3. I am looking at (*progressive*) these magazines. ....

....

4. They are waiting for (*progressive*) the bus. ....

....

5. They are waiting for Diana. ....

....

VII. Write in Spanish:

1. On entering the library, Henrietta sees her friend Rita. ....

....

2. Henrietta greets her: "Hello, Rita! What brings you (*fam. sing.*) here so early?" ....

....

....

3. "You (*fam. sing.*) forget that I wish to enter the School of Medicine; I have a great deal to study."

....

....

4. Although Rita is always very busy, we are sure that she goes out occasionally with her friends.

....

....

5. In the evening she watches television after having supper. ....

....

....

6. Why does Rita want to study that career? She knows that she is going to earn a lot of money.

....

....

7. On arriving at Raymond's house, Thomas knocks at the door. ....

....

8. Raymond opens it and then invites his friend to enter. ....

....

9. Thomas comes from Diane's (house); Diane is Mary's sister. ....

....

....

10. Mary is working in Buenos Aires, but she is on a visit in this country now. ....

....

....

11. I don't know Diane, but I see her often when she leaves her house. ....

....

....

12. Diane lives in that yellow house that we can see through this window. ....

....

....

VIII. Write answers to these questions, using complete sentences:

1. ¿A qué hora sale Ud. de su casa por la mañana?

....

2. ¿Cuántas clases tiene Ud. por la tarde?

....

3. ¿Qué trae Ud. generalmente a la clase de español?

....

4. ¿Escucha Ud. programas de radio en español?

....

5. Al salir de clase, ¿charla Ud. unos momentos con sus amigos?

....

6. ¿Hay una Facultad de Derecho en esta universidad?

....

Lección 7

I. Dictation

The teacher will read two or three exchanges from the dialogues.

....

....

....

....

....

Compare what you have written with your Text, p. 102.

II. Pronunciation exercise

Review the pronunciation of the dipthongs **ai (ay)** and **oi (oy)**, and **ua** and **au** (Text, p. 104); then rewrite the following words and phrases, dividing them into syllables and underlining the stressed syllables:

ochenta y tres ....

Hablo inglés. ....

Hay más ahí. ....

su acción ....

hoy día ....

para usar ....

III. Use of indirect object pronouns

A. Supply the indirect object pronoun which corresponds to the indirect object, following the model.

MODEL: Yo .... doy el libro a Silvia.   *Yo le doy el libro a Silvia.*

1. La vendedora .... enseña varias faldas a Lupe y a Silvia.

2. Ellas .... preguntan a la vendedora si se venden a precio especial.

3. La vendedora .... contesta a las jóvenes que tienen precio fijo en esa tienda.

4. A Lupe .... parece muy cara la falda azul.

5. Silvia .... dice a Lupe que necesita cobrar un cheque.

6. Luego Silvia .... da el dinero a la vendedora.

B. Write affirmative answers to these questions:

1. ¿Te mandan la revista por avión?

....

2. ¿Le escriben a Ud. en español?

....

3. ¿Te mandan dinero tus padres?

....

4. ¿Les venden a Uds. el cuadro?

....

5. ¿Les parece a Uds. barato el reloj?

....

6. ¿Les dicen a Uds. la verdad?

....

IV. Use of *gustar*

Complete with the present indicative tense of **gustar**:

1. Nos .... la lengua española. 2. No me .... esta tienda.

3. Me .... esas dos faldas. 4. A las jóvenes les .... el vestido blanco.

5. No nos .... estos zapatos. 6. ¿Te .... ir de compras? 7. ¿Les

.... a Uds. estas blusas? 8. A los muchachos les .... los programas de

radio. 9. Me .... estudiar por la mañana. 10. A los estudiantes les .... las

vacaciones.

V. Comparison of adjectives

Write affirmative answers, following the model:

MODEL: ¿Es nueva la tienda?   *Sí, es la más nueva de todas.*

1. ¿Es largo el viaje? ....

2. ¿Son fáciles las lecciones? ....

3. ¿Es caro el sombrero? ....

4. ¿Son baratos los libros? ....

5. ¿Es difícil el ejercicio? ....

6. ¿Son bonitas las chicas? ....

VI. Use of se with a verb to substitute for the passive

Rewrite the following sentences using **se** with the corresponding form of the verb, following the model.

MODEL: Aquí hablan español.   *Aquí se habla español.*

1. Necesitan mucho tiempo. ....

2. Venden muchas cosas allí. ....

3. Usan mucho ese libro. ....

4. Hablan varias lenguas aquí. ....

5. Reciben esa revista en casa. ....

6. Abren las puertas temprano. ....

7. Mandan las cartas por avión. ....

8. Compran la ropa en el centro. ....

VII. Write out the numerals and nouns in Spanish:

1. 75 cents ....

2. 49 dollars ....

3. 51 books ....

4. 91 girls ....

5. 43 chairs ....

6. 38 boys ....

7. 77 tickets ....

8. 66 days ....

VIII. Write in Spanish:

1. Sylvia is spending (the) Thanksgiving Day vacation in San Diego. ....

....

....

2. Lupe, one of her classmates, lives with her parents in Tijuana. ....

....

3. On Friday morning Sylvia telephones (calls) her friend Lupe. ....

....

4. After chatting a while, Sylvia tells Lupe that she needs to buy several things. ....

....

....

5. Lupe then invites her to go shopping in Tijuana, because (the) things are cheaper there. ....

....

....

6. Sylvia replies: "Gladly. I'll see you (*fam. sing.*) tomorrow. I'll be there at 11 A.M." ....

....

....

7. On Saturday Sylvia goes to her friend's house. ....

....

8. The two young ladies arrive downtown at about twelve o'clock. ....

....

....

9. They have lunch in a small restaurant on Constitution Street. ....

....

....

10. Afterwards they enter a large store where many dresses, shoes, skirts, and blouses are seen in the

show windows. ....

....

....

11. Lupe tells the saleslady that they want to see the blouses that are on sale (that are sold at (a) special

price). ....

....

....

12. The saleslady shows them several blouses; Sylvia thinks that the white blouse is the prettiest of all.

....

....

IX. Write answers to these questions, using complete sentences:

1. ¿Tiene Ud. que ir al centro hoy?

....

2. ¿A qué hora se abren las tiendas en esta ciudad?

....

3. ¿Cuánto tiempo se necesita para llegar al centro?

....

4. ¿Tiene Ud. que cobrar un cheque hoy?

....

5. ¿Le gusta a Ud. ir de compras?

....

6. ¿Tienen precio fijo en la librería de la universidad?

....

7. ¿Va Ud. a llamar por teléfono a sus padres hoy?

....

8. ¿Qué expresiones se usan para contestar el teléfono?

....

Lección 8

I. Dictation

The teacher will read two or three exchanges from the dialogues.

....

....

....

....

....

Compare what you have written with your Text, p. 116.

II. Pronunciation exercises

A. Review the sounds of **m** and **n** (Text, p. 117); then circle each **n** that is pronounced like **m**:

encontrar	invitar	con papel	son baratos
cansado	son verdes	con Mario	un vestido

B. Review the pronunciation of the diphthongs **ue** and **eu** (Text, p. 118); then rewrite the following words and phrases, dividing them into syllables and underlining the stressed syllables:

cincuenta ....   ¿puede usted? ....

vuelven ....   ¿quiere usted? ....

III. Write the corresponding form of the present indicative tense:

encontrar: yo ....   Ana y yo ....

hacer: Uds. ....   yo   ....

volver: él ....   él y yo   ....

lavarse: yo ....   ellos   ....

          él ....   nosotros ....

pensar: tú ....   Uds.   ....

ponerse: yo ....   nosotros ....

          tú ....   ellos ....

sentarse: yo ....   Uds. ....

          Ud. ....   nosotros ....

IV. Complete with the corresponding form of the present indicative tense of the verb:

1. (almorzar)   Ellos .... en el restaurante.

2. (volver)   Yo .... a casa a las once.

3. (cerrar)   El profesor .... la puerta.

4. (pensar)   ¿..................... tú hacer un viaje pronto?

5. (costar)   ¿Cuánto .... el boleto de avión?

6. (encontrar)   Mario me .... en la cafetería.

7. (desayunarse)   Yo siempre .... temprano.

8. (llamarse)   ¿Cómo .... tu profesora?

9. (sonar)   Cuando .... el teléfono, Ana lo contesta.

10. (ponerse)   ¿Por qué no .... tú los zapatos nuevos?

11. (sentarse)   Jaime y yo .... para escribir el anuncio.

12. (acostarse)   Mi compañero de viaje .... tarde.

13. (lavarse)   Los chicos .... la cara y las manos.

14. (gustar)   ¿Le .... a Ud. viajar en tren?

15. (parecer)   ¿Te .... difíciles estas frases?

16. (parecer)   ¿Qué te .... si salimos el domingo?

V. Rewrite each of the following sentences, placing the reflexive pronoun in the correct position:

1. (me)   Acuesto temprano. No pienso acostar tarde. ....

....

2. (se)   Jaime levanta a las seis. Hoy va a levantar a las siete. ....

....

3. (nos)   Sentamos aquí. No queremos sentar al lado de Jaime. ....

....

4. (nos) ¿Dónde lavamos? ¿No podemos lavar aquí? ....

....

5. (se) Ellos desayunan tarde. No desean desayunar todavía. ....

....

6. (me) Yo pongo las gafas. Yo tengo que poner las gafas. ....

....

7. (se) Ana prepara para salir. Necesita preparar para la clase. ....

....

8. (te) ¿Por qué sientas allí? Puedes sentar cerca de la ventana. ....

....

VI. Write in Spanish:

1. James' parents are from Mexico, but they are living now in Los Angeles. ....

....

2. James tells his friend Mario that he wants to spend Christmas vacation with his family. ....

....

....

3. He is worried because the trip is long and gasoline costs a lot nowadays. ....

....

4. He can't make the trip by plane because he doesn't have enough money. ....

....

5. Mario tells him that he can find a traveling companion if he puts an ad in the newspaper.

....

....

6. After eating breakfast, James and Mario write the ad. ....

....

7. Then they take it to the newspaper office (office of the newspaper). ....

....

8. On the following day, Michael Ramos, a student of the Engineering School, calls James.

....

....

9. Michael tells him that he too is looking for a companion to travel to Los Angeles. ....

....

....

10. James is very happy when Michael says that he wants to leave on Saturday morning. ....

....

....

11. If they leave early, they can visit the mission at (in) Carmel. ....

....

12. Friday evening James goes to bed early (in order) to get ready for the trip. ....

....

....

VII. Write answers to these questions, using complete sentences:

1. ¿Cómo se llama Ud.? ¿Y su profesor (profesora)?

....

2. ¿A qué hora se levanta Ud. generalmente?

....

3. ¿Almuerza Ud. antes o después de las doce?

....

4. ¿A qué hora se acuesta Ud. los sábados?

....

5 ¿Le gusta a Ud. pasar las vacaciones de Navidad con su familia?

....

6. ¿Cuánto cuesta poner un anuncio en el periódico?

....

Lectura 2

A. List the words in the Lectura, Text, pp. 130–131, whose English equivalents (in the singular) lack Spanish final **-a, -e, -o.** Include words which have the additional difference of a written accent, such as **público,** or a single consonant instead of a double one, such as **diferente.**

....

....

....

....

....

....

B. Read each sentence carefully. If the statement is correct, rewrite it, beginning your sentence with "**Sí.**" If the statement is incorrect, correct it, beginning your sentence with "**No**" and making the necessary changes:

1. En cultura y en lengua, México difiere mucho de su vecino al norte del río Grande. ....

....

....

2. Montañas y mesetas ocupan la mayor parte de México. ....

....

3. El sur de México es un gran desierto. ....

....

4. La mayor parte de los mexicanos viven en la meseta central. ....

....

5. La ciudad de México es el centro comercial y cultural del país. ....

....

6. Muchas de las colonias de la capital tienen avenidas anchas y casas nuevas de arquitectura moderna.

....

....

43

7. La ciudad de Guadalajara es un puerto importante en la costa del Golfo de México. ....

   ....

8. La riqueza de México es principalmente agrícola y minera. ....

   ....

9. Más de la mitad de la población de México se dedica a la producción de petróleo. ....

   ....

10. A pesar de su riqueza agrícola y minera, México sufre actualmente una crisis económica muy seria.

    ....

    ....

11. La civilización del país es una mezcla de la cultura indígena y de la cultura de los españoles.

    ....

    ....

12. El fenómeno característico que distingue a los mexicanos es la unificación racial. ....

    ....

    ....

Lección 9

I. Dictation

The teacher will read two or three exchanges from the dialogues.

....

....

....

....

....

Compare what you have written with your Text, p. 136.

II. Pronunciation exercises

A. Review the sounds of Spanish **s** (Text, p. 138); then circle each **s** that is pronounced somewhat like English hissed *s* in *sent:*

la música	antes de ir	franceses	les gusta
los meses	las blusas	mismo	usamos

B. Review linking (Text, p. 9), paying special attention to the linking of vowels between words; then rewrite the following sentences, each of which may be considered as one breath group, dividing them into syllables and underlining the stressed syllables:

Escucha a Jaime. ....

Tu amiga habló. ....

Fue un éxito. ....

III. Change each verb form to the preterit tense:

1. Jaime y Miguel (se levantan) .... a las siete. 2. (Se lavan)

.... la cara y las manos. 3. (Entran) .... en el

comedor y (se desayunan) .... 4. Su amigo Carlos (se levanta)

.... tarde y no (toma) .... el desayuno. 5. Jaime y

Miguel lo (esperan) .... un rato. 6. A las ocho menos diez los tres (salen)

.... para la universidad. 7. (Entran) .... en la sala de

clase y (se sientan) .... 8. El profesor (entra) .... y

(saluda) .... a los estudiantes. 9. Ellos (escuchan) ....

sus preguntas y las (contestan) .... en español. 10. Cuando (termina)

.... la clase, algunos de los estudiantes (se quedan) ....

para hablar con el profesor. 11. Otros (van) .... a otras clases. 12. Jaime y

Miguel (vuelven) .... a la residencia.

IV. Write the corresponding form of the present indicative tense:

dar:	yo	....	ellos	....
	tú	....	él y yo	....
ir:	tú	....	Ana y yo	....
	yo	....	Uds.	....
ser:	tú	....	nosotros	....
	él	....	ellos	....
recordar:	yo	....	ella y yo	....
	Ud.	....	ellas	....
quedarse:	tú	....	Uds.	....
	yo	....	nosotros	....

V. Make each sentence negative, following the models.

MODELS: Vemos algo.   *No vemos nada* or *Nada vemos.*
         Alguien viene ahora.   *Nadie viene ahora* or *No viene nadie ahora.*

1. Hay algo en el coche. ....

2. Veo a alguien en la calle. ....

3. Alguno de Uds. contestó. ....

4. Están escribiendo algo. ....

5. Conozco a alguna de las chicas. ....

6. Uds. siempre vienen tarde. ....

7. Ella siempre me da algo. ....

8. Lola se quedó también. ....

9. Laura encontró algo allí. ....

10. Tomás va a clase también. ....

11. Alguien baila ahora. ....

12. Alguna de tus tías llamó. ....

VI. Supply the corresponding definite article when necessary:

1. Jorge llegó .... viernes por .... noche. 2. Él no mira muchos programas de ....

televisión. 3. ¿A qué hora toma Ud. .... desayuno? ¿A .... ocho? 4. Hoy es .... lunes.

5. Ayer fue .... domingo. 6. Lola lleva .... bolsa en .... mano. 7. .... alemán es

una lengua difícil. 8. ¿Por qué no te pones .... zapatos? 9. ¿Te gusta .... invierno?

10. Buenas tardes, ... señor Molina. 11. .... señorita López viene todos .... días.

12. Ella y .... señor Ortega son profesores de .... Argentina. 13. Yo los visité ....

semana pasada. 14. ¿Te gustan .... películas norteamericanas? 15. ¿Te lavaste .... manos y

.... cara? 16. Ellos piensan salir .... martes que viene. 17. ¿Fueron Uds. al concierto

.... mes pasado? 18. Pensamos pasar .... vacaciones de Navidad en .... Uruguay. 19.

Hablan .... español en .... México. 20. Recibí el periódico de .... universidad

.... miércoles.

VII. Write in Spanish:

1. Last year George spent Christmas vacation in Madrid with his family. ....

....

2. One Sunday afternoon he went to a movie, where he met his friend Lola. ....

....

....

3. What a coincidence, Lola! But now I remember that you always liked North American films.

....

....

4. George tried to call her Saturday night, but no one answered. ....

....

5. The film that they are going to see has some fantastic dance numbers. ....

....

6. Lola's cousins (*f.*) saw the film last week with her uncle and aunt. ....

....

7. After this type of film, the fashion of (the) discotheques began. ....

....

8. Lola tells George that she and her friends often go to concerts of Spanish music. ....

....

....

9. Everybody knows that Julio Iglesias is living in the United States now. ....

....

10. He was a "hit" when he gave a concert of Spanish songs in California last year. ....

....

....

11. The film is beginning now, George. Why don't you call me another day? ....

....

12. It is going to be difficult because George is leaving for the United States next Wednesday.

....

....

VIII. Write answers to these questions, using complete sentences:

1. ¿Compró Ud. algo la semana pasada?

....

2. ¿Llamó Ud. por teléfono a alguien anoche?

....

3. ¿Encontró Ud. a alguno de sus amigos en la calle esta mañana?

....

4. ¿Fue Ud. al cine con alguien el domingo pasado?

....

5. ¿Se quedó Ud. en casa el sábado por la noche?

....

6. ¿Dónde pasó Ud. las vacaciones de Navidad el año pasado?

....

....

Lección 10

I. Dictation

The teacher will read two exchanges from the dialogue.

....

....

....

....

....

Compare what you have written with your Text, p. 152.

II. Pronunciation exercises

A. Review the sounds of Spanish **x** (Text, p. 153); then circle each **x** that is pronounced like English *s* in *sent:*

excelente	éxito	expresión	extranjero
mexicano	excursión	examen	exacto

B. Review the pronunciation of Spanish **j** (Text, pp. 56 and 153); then circle each letter that is pronounced like Spanish **j:**

gente	Texas	reloj	ingeniería
Los Ángeles	alguien	México	argentino

III. Write the corresponding form of the imperfect indicative tense:

	yo	nosotros	Uds.
1. contar:	....	....	....
2. hacer:	....	....	....
3. salir:	....	....	....
4. ir:	....	....	....
5. ser:	....	....	....
6. ver:	....	....	....

IV. Rewrite each of the following sentences, first changing the verb to the preterit indicative tense, and then to the imperfect tense:

1. Yo vuelvo del campo.
   ....

   ....

2. Jaime los ve.
   ....

   ....

3. Ud. cierra la puerta.
   ....

   ....

4. Vamos a la playa.
   ....

   ....

5. Jaime habla de su niñez.
   ....

   ....

6. Ella cuenta su dinero.
   ....

   ....

7. Tomás corre por el camino.
   ....

   ....

8. Escribimos los ejercicios.
   ....

   ....

V. Complete, using the correct form of the imperfect indicative tense of *estar, haber, hacer,* or *ser,* as required:

1. Como .... invierno, ... mucho frío. 2. .... mucho viento

también. 3. Aunque .... despejado, ... lodo por todas partes.

4. .... mal tiempo. 5. .... niebla en las montañas. 6. ....

fresco, y .... nubes en el cielo. 7. .... un día hermoso de verano.

8. El café .... frío. 9. El agua no .... caliente. 10. ¿Dónde vivía Ud.

cuando .... pequeño? 11. Mis abuelos .... españoles. 12. ....

la una de la tarde.

VI. Complete with the corresponding form of the preterit or imperfect indicative tense, as required:

1. Como Jaime y Miguel no (desear) .... llegar a Los Ángeles de noche, (decidir) .... salir muy temprano. 2. No (ser) .... todavía las cinco cuando Jaime (llamar) .... a la puerta de la residencia donde (vivir) .... Miguel. 3. Aunque (hacer) .... fresco a esa hora, no (hacer) .... mal tiempo. 4. Miguel (estar) .... seguro de que en Los Ángeles (haber) .... sol. 5. A Miguel no le (gustar) .... el invierno aquí. 6. Jaime siempre (recordar) .... la vida en el Caribe, donde la gente seguramente (estar) .... gozando del sol. 7. Los padres de Miguel (ser) .... mexicanos; (vivir) .... en un pueblo cerca de Los Ángeles. 8. Miguel (hablar) .... español con sus abuelos, que ya (ser) .... muy viejos. 9. La familia de Jaime (ser) .... cubana; cuando (ser) .... necesario salir de Cuba, sus padres (comprar) .... una casa en Los Ángeles. 10. Cuando (entrar) .... en la ciudad, (comenzar) .... a llover. 11. (Haber) .... muchas nubes en el cielo; (estar) .... nublado. 12. Miguel (llevar) .... a Jaime a su casa y después (ir) .... a (la) casa de sus padres.

VII. Write in Spanish:

1. It was cloudy when James and Michael left for Los Angeles by car. ....

....

....

2. While they were having lunch in Monterey, it began to rain. ....

....

....

3. But when they arrived at Los Angeles, the weather was good (it was good weather) and the sun was

shining. ....

....

4. During the trip Michael told James many things about his family. ....

....

....

5. His grandfather left Mexico because he hoped to earn more money in the United States. ....

....

....

6. When Michael was small, his family used to live in a town near the border. ....

....

....

7. His father learned to speak and write English and studied at the university. ....

....

....

8. Michael would always bring things to his brothers and sisters when he visited his family. ....

....

....

9. During the summer his family liked to go on an excursion to the mountains. ....

....

....

10. They would also go often to a beach that was not far from their house. ....

....

....

11. It was quite late when the two young men arrived at Los Angeles. ....

....

....

12. James invited his friend to have something to drink and to rest a while before taking him to his

home. ....

....

VIII. Write answers to these questions, using complete sentences:

1. ¿Hace mal tiempo hoy?

   ....

2. ¿Hace calor o frío hoy?

   ....

3. ¿Hay sol ahora?

   ....

4. ¿Estaba nublado o despejado esta mañana?

   ....

5. ¿Hay nubes en el cielo ahora?

   ....

6. ¿Qué tiempo hace aquí en el invierno?

   ....

7. ¿Por qué es agradable la primavera en algunas partes del país?

   ....

8. ¿Hace mucho viento aquí en el mes de mayo?

   ....

Lección 11

I. Dictation

The teacher will read two or three exchanges from the dialogue.

....

....

....

....

....

....

Compare what you have written with your Text, p. 170.

II. Pronunciation exercise

Review the principles that govern the pronunciation of the conjunction **y** (Text, p. 172); then rewrite the following sentences as single breath groups, dividing them into syllables, underlining the stressed syllables, and using linking signs to connect consonants and vowels which should be pronounced in a single syllable:

Sabe inglés y francés. ....

Usted y Elena van. ....

Habla y escribe bien. ....

Es azul y amarillo. ....

III. Commands and object pronouns

A. Rewrite each sentence, placing the object pronoun in the correct position:

1. (la)   Elena abre. No quiere abrir. Abra Ud. No abra Ud. ....

....

....

2. (los)   Ana trae. No puede traer. Traiga Ud. No traiga Ud. ....

....

....

3. (las)   Ellos cierran. Van a cerrar. Cierren Uds. No cierren Uds. ....

....

....

4. (se)   Antonio lava. Promete lavar. Lave Ud. No lave Ud. ....

....

....

B. Answer the following questions with formal singular commands in the affirmative and in the negative, using pronouns for the noun objects:

1. ¿Visito a Miguel? ....

....

2. ¿Vendo el coche? ....

....

3. ¿Hago el viaje? ....

....

4. ¿Pongo el anuncio? ....

....

C. Write in Spanish, using formal commands:

1. I invite Lola. I want to invite her. Invite (sing.) her. Don't invite her. ....

....

2. George writes the ad. He writes it. Write (sing.) it. Don't write it. ....

....

3. We take a trip. We take it. Take (pl.) it. Don't take it. ....

....

4. We give the money. We plan to give it. Give (pl.) it. Don't give it. ....

....

IV. Complete, using the present indicative tense of *estar, hacer, ser,* or *tener:*

1. .... mal tiempo hoy. 2. ¿No .... Ud. mucho frío? 3. Laura

.... mucho sueño. 4. Ella .... muy cansada también. 5. El café

no .... muy caliente. 6. El agua .... muy fría.

7. Hoy .... jueves. 8. Ya .... las dos de la tarde. 9. Creo

que .... el cumpleaños de Ana. 10. .... necesario celebrarlo.

11. ¿De qué color .... la silla? 12. ¿Cuántos años .... ella?

13. .... nublado hoy. 14. Las nubes .... bonitas.

15. Como .... sol, yo .... mucho calor.

16. María .... sed.

V. Ways to express "time"

Complete with **hora, rato, tiempo, vez,** or **veces,** as required:

1. ¿Adónde van Uds. a esta .... de la tarde? 2. Estas chicas nunca llegan

a .... 3. Los estudiantes pasan un .... aquí todas las tardes.

4. A .... preparamos empanadas. 5. Vemos a Ramón de .... en

cuando. 6. Queremos descansar un .... ahora. 7. No tengo .... para

ir al banco. 8. ¿A qué .... comienza la clase? 9. Los jóvenes charlan todo

el .... 10. ¿Quieren Uds. traer unos discos esta .... ?

VI. Write in Spanish:

1. One afternoon Helen and Margaret were returning to their room after having lunch. ....

....

....

2. When they were opening the door, the telephone rang. ....

....

....

3. Helen left her books on a chair and ran to answer it. ....

....

4. Anthony, a Chilean student, wanted to know whether he could speak to Margaret. ....

    ....

    ....

5. He wanted to invite the two girls to a birthday party for (**para**) Charles. ....

    ....

    ....

6. Helen didn't know that they were planning to celebrate Charles' birthday. ....

    ....

    ....

7. Anthony thinks that Charles is going to be nineteen years old. ....

    ....

8. Helen wants to know what they can take to the party. ....

    ....

9. Anthony replies: "Think (*pl.*) of some typical dish of your countries." ....

    ....

    ....

10. Helen promises to prepare (a) guacamole (salad); Margaret is going to bring some drinks.

    ....

    ....

11. The boys intend to prepare turnovers, flan, and a Valencian paella. ....

    ....

    ....

12. Then Anthony says: "George tells me that you (*pl.*) have some new records that we can play; don't

    forget to bring them." ....

    ....

    ....

VII. Write affirmative answers to these questions, adding the correct equivalent for English "very" in your answer, as in the model.

MODEL: ¿Tiene Ud. frío?   *Sí, tengo mucho frío.*

1. ¿Tiene Ud. calor?

....

2. ¿Tiene Ud. sueño también?

....

3. ¿Tienes hambre todavía?

....

4. ¿Tienen sed Elena y Margarita?

....

5. ¿Está fría el agua?

....

6. ¿Está caliente el café?

....

7. ¿Hace fresco aquí en la primavera?

....

8. ¿Hay sol aquí en el invierno?

....

Lección 12

I. Dictation

The teacher will read the first three exchanges from the dialogue.

....

....

....

....

....

....

Compare what you have written with your Text, p. 184.

II. Pronunciation exercise

Review word stress and linking (Text, pp. 6, 8, and 92); then rewrite the next to the last exchange of the dialogue of this lesson, dividing the four sentences into breath groups and into syllables, and underlining the stressed syllables. Remember that conjunctions (**pues, y, pero, si**), prepositions (**a**), reflexive pronouns (**se**), and the forms of the definite article are pronounced as unstressed words in Spanish.

....

....

....

....

III. Rewrite the following sentences, changing each conjugated verb first to the preterit tense, and then to the imperfect indicative tense:

1. Jorge dice la verdad.   ....

   ....

2. Yo no quiero subir.   ....

   ....

3. Venimos a verte. ....

....

4. Él nos hace ese favor. ....

....

IV. Rewrite each of the following sentences, placing the object pronouns in their correct position:

1. (lo)   Ellos hicieron. No quisieron hacer. Están haciendo.

....

....

2. (las)   Elena saca. Va a sacar. Está sacando.

....

....

3. (la)   Yo escribí. Prometí escribir. Yo estaba escribiendo.

....

....

4. (me)   Tomás contesta. Conteste Ud. Él trata de contestar.

....

....

V. Rewrite each sentence, using the progressive form of the verb and substituting the correct object pronoun for each noun object. Follow the models.

MODEL: Ramón escucha la canción.   *Ramón está escuchándola.*

1. Jorge toca el disco. ....

2. Lola hace el flan. ....

3. La criada busca las llaves. ....

4. Todos leen la noticia. ....

MODEL: Margarita charla con Mario.   *Margarita está charlando con él.*

5. Mario no estudia con Laura. ....

6. Ella viaja sin su esposo. ....

64

7. Compro algo para mi madre. ....

8. Jorge corre al lado de Tomás. ....

VI. Rewrite each sentence, changing it to the reflexive construction with se.

MODEL: Cierran la puerta a las seis.   *Se cierra la puerta a las seis.*

1. Pueden entrar por aquí.

....

2. Comen bien en este restaurante.

....

3. Dicen que no hay clase hoy.

....

4. ¿Toman dinero norteamericano aquí?

....

VII. Write out the numerals in Spanish:

1. (101) .... cuartos.

2. (200) .... sillas.

3. (500) .... libros.

4. (450) .... boletos.

5. (1,000) .... hombres.

6. (665) .... programas.

7. (991) .... palabras.

8. (2,400) .... dólares.

9. (1,300,000) .... pesetas.

10. (3,000,000) .... de personas.

VIII. Write in Spanish, following the model.

MODEL: May 3, 1984   el tres de mayo de mil novecientos ochenta y cuatro

1. April 15, 1970 ....

....

2. January 1, 1985 ....

....

3. February 22, 1732 ....

....

4. May 2, 1808 ....

....

5. September 16, 1810 ....

....

6. December 25, 1958 ....

....

7. October 12, 1492 ....

....

8. August 14, 1556 ....

....

IX. Write in Spanish:

1. In 1975 Mr. and Mrs. Ramos traveled in (**por**) Spain by train. ....

....

....

2. This time they are traveling by car because that way one sees the country better. ....

....

....

3. Since Mr. Ramos' parents were Spanish, it is important for them to know Spain well. ....

....

....

4. Wishing to visit Cordova again (*use* **volver a**), they decided to spend a day there. ....

....

....

5. Although they didn't make reservations, they found a good hotel in the center of the city.

....

....

6. Their friends told them that it wasn't necessary to make reservations at this time of the year.

....

....

7. The receptionist told them that there was a room with two beds and bath on the second floor.

....

....

8. Mrs. Ramos asked the receptionist whether they could see the room. ....

....

....

9. Taking the elevator, they went up to the room, which had windows that faced the square.

....

....

10. The view of the square, where many people were strolling, was very nice. ....

....

....

11. They decided to take the room, and Mr. Ramos went down to the first (main) floor to register.

....

....

12. The receptionist gave them the keys and told them that the dining room closed (was closed) at

11:00 P.M. ....

....

....

X. Write answers to these questions, using complete sentences:

1. ¿Qué fecha es hoy?

   ....

2. ¿Qué día de la semana es?

   ....

3. ¿Qué día de la semana fue ayer?

   ....

4. ¿Qué mes es?

   ....

5. ¿Cuántos días hay en este mes?

   ....

6. ¿Cuántos días hay en un año?

   ....

Lectura 3

A. List the words in the *Lectura*, Text, pp. 198–200, whose English equivalents (in the singular) lack the Spanish final **-a, -e, -o.** Include words which have the additional difference of a written accent or a single consonant instead of a double one:

....

....

....

....

....

....

B. Identify briefly in Spanish—in a word or phrase—the place name or common noun to which each of the following refers:

1. Tres de las seis repúblicas hispanoamericanas que se encuentran entre México y Colombia.

  ....

2. Es tropical en las costas y tierras bajas de Centroamérica. ....

  ....

3. La base de la economía de la región. ....

  ....

4. Los productos principales de la región. ....

  ....

5. La base de una importante industria en Costa Rica. ....

  ....

6. Una de las flotas mercantes más importantes del mundo. ....

  ....

7. Dos repúblicas hispanoamericanas que se encuentran en el Mar Caribe. ....

  ....

8. Una de las primeras naciones del mundo en la producción de azúcar. ....

....

9. El origen de muchas canciones y muchos bailes que son muy populares en nuestro país. ....

....

10. La primera ciudad creada por los españoles en el Nuevo Mundo. ....

....

11. La isla que en 1952 se declaró estado libre, associado a los Estados Unidos. ....

....

12. El origen de muchos habitantes en todas las islas del Mar Caribe. ....

....

Lección 13

I. Dictation

The teacher will read two or three exchanges from the dialogues.

....

....

....

....

....

....

Compare what you have written with your Text, p. 204.

II. Complete with the corresponding form of the preterit indicative tense:

1. (llegar)   Yo .... a Cozumel anoche.

2. (tener)   Yo .... tiempo para ir de compras.

3. (buscar)   Esta mañana yo .... unos regalos para mis hermanos.

4. (envolver)   El dependiente .... los artículos que compré.

5. (entregar)   Después, él me .... el paquete.

6. (pagar)   Al salir de la tienda, yo .... la cuenta.

7. (poder)   Nosotros .... descansar en la playa también.

8. (estar)   ¿Cuánto tiempo .... la señora Ramos en la isla?

9. (preguntar)   ¿........................... ella por una joyería típica?

10. (enseñar)   ¿Qué le .... los dependientes?

III. Rewrite each sentence, using the correct command forms:

1. (Tocar) Ud. este disco.   ....

2. No (comenzar) Ud. todavía.   ....

3. (Buscar) Uds. otra pulsera. ....

4. (Entregar) Ud. el dinero. ....

5. No (cruzar) Uds. la calle. ....

6. (Llegar) Uds. a tiempo, por favor. ....

IV. Rewrite each sentence, substituting the corresponding demonstrative pronoun for the demonstrative adjective and noun in italics:

1. ¿De quién es *este disco*? ....

2. Me llevo *esa guayabera*. ....

3. Envuelva Ud. *estos ceniceros*. ....

4. *Aquellos cinturones* son caros. ....

5. *Estas carteras* son de cuero. ....

6. *Esos aretes* son muy finos. ....

V. Rewrite each sentence, substituting the correct object pronoun for each noun and article in italics, and placing it in the correct position:

1. Ella me vendió *los anillos*. ....

2. Le devolví *el cinturón*. ....

3. Yo me llevé *los aretes*. ....

4. ¿Se compró Clara *el collar*? ....

5. Lupe se puso *las joyas*. ....

6. Póngase Ud. *los zapatos*. ....

7. No les dé Ud. *los regalos*. ....

8. No pude traerle *el paquete*. ....

9. Están lavándome *el coche*. ....

10. Acabo de decirle *la verdad*. ....

VI. Write in Spanish, using the formal singular form for "you":

1. The bill. Bring it to me; don't show it to Martha.

....

72

2. The ring. I want to return it to them; hand it to them, please.

....

....

3. The blouses. Ann has just bought them; she is taking them with her.

....

....

4. The tickets. Look for them; I want to give them to them (*f. pl.*).

....

VII. Write in Spanish:

1. Last winter Mr. and Mrs. Ramos were able to take a trip to Yucatan. ....

....

....

2. They were in Cozumel several days, resting quietly. ....

....

3. They enjoyed the beautiful beaches and they also had time to go shopping. ....

....

....

4. One afternoon, being downtown, they entered a jewelry shop. ....

....

....

5. They wanted to buy some Mexican articles for their children. ....

....

....

6. Mrs. Ramos asked the clerk: "Can you show us some gold earrings?" ....

....

....

7. In one of the showcases there were beautiful earrings of many styles. ....

....

....

8. The clerk also showed them pins that matched the earrings. ....

....

....

9. Mrs. Ramos put on some earrings that looked great on her. ....

....

....

10. When she said that she liked them, her husband bought them for her at once. ....

....

11. After paying the bill, they went to the market to look for some pieces of pottery for their friends.

....

....

12. After a short while Mr. Ramos told his wife that he wanted to buy some guayaberas for Michael.

....

....

VIII. Write answers to these questions, using complete sentences:

1. ¿Va Ud. de compras a menudo?

....

2. ¿Hay tiendas grandes cerca de la universidad?

....

3. ¿Dónde pueden comprarse joyas?

....

4. ¿Cuáles son algunas joyas que les gustan a las señoritas?

....

5. ¿Qué artículos para las señoritas pueden comprarse en México?

   ....

6. ¿Cuándo compra Ud. regalos para sus amigos y amigas?

   ....

7. ¿Dónde se venden libros, plumas y papel?

   ....

8. ¿Qué nos pregunta el dependiente cuando entramos en una tienda?

   ....

   ....

Lección 14

I. Dictation

The teacher will read two or three exchanges from the dialogue.

....

....

....

....

....

....

Compare what you have written with your Text, p. 220.

II. Complete with the corresponding form of the present perfect indicative tense:

1. (hallar)   Nosotros no .... tus llaves.

2. (vender)   Ellos .... algunos de sus libros.

3. (disfrutar) Yo.. mucho de las vacaciones.

4. (devolver)   ¿Nos .... él el paquete?

5. (escribir)   ¿Les .... tú una tarjeta?

6. (ver)   Ellos .... pueblos encantadores.

7. (sentarse)   Los jóvenes .... en la arena.

8. (ponerse)   Nosotros .... muy bronceados.

9. (ir)   Se cree que mi tío .... a pescar.

10. (estar)   Yo .... en la playa.

Complete with the corresponding form of the pluperfect indicative tense:

11. (decir)   Ellas .... que no querían bucear hoy.

12. (volver)   Tu madre no .... de la peluquería.

13. (oír)   ¿ .... tú las palabras del profesor?

14. (abrir)   No se .... las tiendas todavía.

III. Use of *hace,* meaning "ago, since"

Write two answers to each pair of questions, following the model.

MODEL: ¿Cuándo llegó Ud.? ¿Hace una hora?   *Sí, llegué hace una hora.*
                                                Sí, hace una hora que llegué.

1. ¿Cuándo salió Clara? ¿Hace quince minutos? ....

   ....

2. ¿Cuándo volvieron Uds.? ¿Hace dos semanas? ....

   ....

3. ¿Cuándo la vio Ud.? ¿Hace dos horas? ....

   ....

4. ¿Cuándo se arregló ella el pelo? ¿Hace un par de días? ....

   ....

IV. Write the Spanish for:

1. Please *(formal sing.)* call *(use* avisar) Mr. Ramos.

   ....

2. I can't hear anything.

   ....

3. Neither can I. Speak *(formal sing.)* louder, please.

   ....

4. One must wait a while.

   ....

5. What's new? How was the trip?

   ....

6. In short, we have been fortunate.

   ....

78

7. We have gotten quite tanned.

   ....

8. How fantastic to scuba dive here!

   ....

V. Write in Spanish:

1. Since this is the last day of their vacation, Mr. and Mrs. Ramos have gone to the beach early.

   ....

   ....

2. Mr. Ramos had put on his bathing suit and had swum a lot. ....

   ....

   ....

3. Since they intended to leave on the next day, Mrs. Ramos wanted to have her hair done.

   ....

   ....

4. She had just left the room when the telephone rang. ....

   ....

5. Michael asks his father: "When did you (*fam. sing.*) return to your room?" "A quarter of an hour

   ago." ....

   ....

   ....

6. Michael was worried because he had not had news of them. ....

   ....

7. He asks his father how things have gone. ....

   ....

8. Mr. Ramos replies that they are well and that they have enjoyed their vacation a lot. ....

   ....

   ....

9. When Michael asks whether the beaches are pretty, his father answers: "You must see them, son!" ....

....

10. Michael also wanted to know whether his father had gone fishing. ....

....

11. His father had written him several cards telling (*use* **contar**) him about the fishing there.

....

....

12. The two could not hear well; there were people who were chatting in the hall. ....

....

....

VI. Write answers to these questions, using complete sentences:

1. ¿En qué meses del año es agradable ir a la playa?

....

2. ¿Cuántas veces ha ido Ud. a la playa este año?

....

3. ¿Ha estado Ud. alguna vez en Cozumel?

....

4. ¿Le gusta a Ud. nadar en el mar?

....

5. ¿Cuántos años tenía Ud. cuando aprendió a nadar?

....

6. ¿Le interesa a Ud. aprender a bucear?

....

7. ¿Se pone Ud. bronceado (bronceada) durante el verano?

....

8. ¿Adónde va uno para arreglarse el pelo?

....

NAME ....

SECTION ....

DATE ....

Lectura 4

A. Give English cognates for the following words in the *Lectura*, Text, pp. 232–233.

montaña   ....   famoso   ....

desierto   ....   industria   ....

norte   ....   economía   ....

fértil   ....   costa   ....

petróleo   ....   centro   ....

respectivamente ....   eliminar   ....

B. Complete each of the following sentences:

1. En Suramérica hay nueve repúblicas en que se habla ....

2. El continente tiene montañas, llanuras, ...

   ....

3. Venezuela es un país muy rico en ....

4. La riqueza principal de Colombia es el ....

5. Además de Colombia, las repúblicas de la costa del Océano Pacífico son el Ecuador, ...

   ....

6. Las bases de la economía del Perú son la industria minera y ....

   ....

7. El Ecuador ha llegado a ser la primera nación del mundo en la ....

   ....

8. La base de la riqueza y de la economía de Chile es la ....

   ....

9. Las bases de la economía de la Argentina son la ....

   ....

10. La capital y el puerto principal del Uruguay es ....

11. Bolivia y el Paraguay están en el ....

12. La América del Sur no ha progresado con la rapidez deseada, a pesar de ....

....

Lección 15

I. Dictation

The teacher will read two or three exchanges from the dialogue.

....

....

....

....

....

....

Compare what you have written with your Text, p. 240.

II. Complete with the corresponding form of the verb, as indicated:

(Future) 1. Alberto le pregunta a Jorge si se (mostrar) .... un partido de

fútbol en la televisión esa tarde. 2. Jorge contesta que (poder) .... decírselo

después de mirar la guía. 3. Hojeando la guía, Jorge ve que (haber) ....

un partido importante. 4. Le pregunta a su compañero qué hora (ser) ....

5. El programa (comenzar) .... a las dos en punto.

6. (Jugar) .... los equipos de Italia y Alemania.

7. Alberto está seguro de que (ser) .... un partido muy emocionante.

8. Pronto (saber) .... los muchachos dónde se juega el partido.

(Conditional) 9. ¿Te (gustar) .... comer con nosotros mañana? 10. Luis

dijo que él y su compañero de cuarto (venir) .... también. 11. ¿(Poder)

.... tú venir a eso de las seis? 12. Nos (alegrar) ....

mucho de verte.

III. Rewrite each sentence according to the model in each group and give the English meaning.

MODEL: ¿Qué hora es?   *¿Qué hora será? What time can it be? (I wonder what time it is.)*

1. Son las cinco. ....

   ....

2. ¿Adónde van las chicas? ....

   ....

3. Tú tienes hambre. ....

   ....

4. Elena quiere descansar. ....

   ....

5. ¿Qué hacen tus compañeros? ....

   ....

6. Ellos están jugando al tenis. ....

   ....

MODEL: ¿Adónde ha ido Lola?   *¿Adónde habrá ido Lola? I wonder where Lola has gone.*

7. ¿Qué han dicho las chicas? ....

   ....

8. Miguel ha pagado la cuenta. ....

   ....

9. Ellos han ido al cine. ....

   ....

10. María se ha desayunado ya. ....

    ....

MODEL: Eran las cinco.   *Serían las cinco. It was probably (must have been, was about) five o'clock.*

11. Elena estaba muy enferma. ....

    ....

84

12. ¿A qué hora volvió Margarita? ....

....

13. ¿Qué compró ella en el centro? ....

....

14. Ellos no sabían la verdad. ....

....

IV. Write in Spanish, using the familiar singular form for "you":

1. It is one o'clock sharp. ....

2. There will be a game today. ....

3. Shall we sit down? ....

4. Shall I turn on the television? ....

5. We are fond of tennis. ....

6. We also like to play golf. ....

7. Did you hear the doorbell? ....

8. They must be at home. ....

9. We have just arrived. ....

10. Would you like to stay here? ....

11. We are glad to be with you. ....

12. You must have seen the game. ....

V. Write in Spanish:

1. One Sunday morning George and Albert are seated in the living room of their apartment. ......

....

2. They have invited Louis, a new Spanish American student, to visit them. ....

....

3. George is turning the pages of the sports section of the newspaper. ....

....

....

4. They will show the final match of the World Cup that morning on television. ....

....

....

5. The two young men don't know where the match is being played. ....

....

6. George thinks that they are going to play the match in one of the stadiums of Madrid. ....

....

....

7. They will soon know, because the game will begin at twelve o'clock. ....

....

....

8. When the doorbell rang, Albert opened the door and Louis came in. ....

....

....

9. They chatted a few minutes and then George went into the kitchen and came back with some soft

drinks. ....

....

10. Louis tells them that he is fond of all (the) sports; when he was in high school, he played tennis and

football. ....

....

....

11. He would like to play tennis more, but there are always a lot of people on the university tennis

courts. ....

....

....

12. George promised to call Louis soon to make a date with him. ....

....

....

VI. Write answers to these questions, using complete sentences:

1. ¿Qué deportes le interesan a Ud. más?

....

2. ¿Ha jugado Ud. al tenis o al golf?

....

3. ¿Ha visto Ud. un partido de fútbol de estilo *soccer*?

....

4. ¿Le gustaría a Ud. jugar en uno de los equipos de la universidad?

....

5. ¿A qué deportes juega Ud. ahora?

....

6. ¿A qué deportes jugaba Ud. en la escuela secundaria?

....

7. ¿Tiene Ud. una bicicleta? ¿Hace Ud. excursiones en bicicleta?

....

8. ¿Ha hecho Ud. excursiones a las montañas este año?

....

Lección 16

I. Commands

A. Change each affirmative command to a negative command:

1. Hazlo esta tarde. ....

2. Dinos el precio del anillo. ....

3. Ve al centro con ellos. ....

4. Saca las fotos hoy. ....

B. Change first to a formal singular command and then to a familiar singular one:

1. Jaime vuelve temprano. ....

....

2. Lupe me trae la pulsera. ....

....

3. Luisa nos dice eso. ....

....

4. Antonio busca al médico. ....

....

C. Answer first with an affirmative singular familiar command, and then with a negative one:

1. ¿Comienzo en seguida? ....

....

2. ¿Los pongo aquí? ....

....

3. ¿Salgo del cuarto? ....

....

4. ¿Duermo la siesta? ....

....

II. Comparison of adjectives

A. Complete with the comparative form of each adjective, following the model.

MODEL: La iglesia es alta.   *Es más alta que aquélla.*

1. Nuestro estadio es pequeño. ....

2. Estos coches son caros. ....

3. El hotel es nuevo. ....

4. Estas flores son hermosas. ....

B. Complete with the superlative form of each adjective (watching for two irregular forms), following the model.

MODEL: La tienda es pequeña.   *Es la más pequeña de todas.*

1. Esta lección es larga. .... de todas.

2. Esos aretes son hermosos. .... de todos.

3. Esta bicicleta es mala. .... de todas.

4. Nuestro equipo es bueno. .... de todos.

C. Rewrite each sentence, using the alternate form of the absolute superlative, following the model.

MODEL: La casa es muy grande.   *La casa es grandísima.*

1. El anillo es muy caro. ....

2. María es muy alta. ....

3. La película es muy mala. ....

4. La ciudad es muy vieja. ....

D. Complete with **tanto, -a, -os, -as,** as required:

1. Rita no ha recibido .... regalos como Ana.

2. El señor Ramos ha comprado .... cosas como su esposa.

3. Jaime no estudió .... horas como Miguel.

· 4. Hoy no hay .... gente en la playa como ayer.

III. Possessive adjectives that follow the noun

A. Rewrite each phrase, substituting **suyo, -a, -os, -as** for the italicized expression, as required:

1. Jaime y dos tíos *de él* ....

2. Miguel y una amiga *de él* ....

3. Clara y dos primas *de ella* ....

4. Ellas y un amigo *de ellas* ....

5. Lupe y dos hermanos *de ella* ....

6. Marta y un primo *de ella* ....

7. Ud. y el profesor *de Ud.* ....

8. Uds. y los padres *de Uds.* ....

B. Write in Spanish, using the familiar singular form for "of yours":

1. this car of mine ....

2. that bicycle of yours ....

3. these suits of mine ....

4. this apartment of ours ....

5. that hat of his ....

6. Helen and an aunt of hers ....

7. that store of theirs ....

8. that idea of yours ....

IV. Write the Spanish for:

1. What's the matter with Ann?

....

2. She doesn't feel well.

....

3. She has a headache (*two ways*).

....

4. She has a very high fever.

....

5. Did you (*pl.*) enjoy yourselves at the dance?

....

6. Finally Ann took a nap.

   ....

7. They must have gone to church.

   ....

8. Laughing, he exclaimed: "Thanks for your (*formal*) patience!"

   ....

V. Write in Spanish:

1. One Sunday afternoon Rita and James went to the university hospital to visit Ann, a good friend of

   theirs. ....

   ....

2. Ann's parents had told them that their friend was ill. ....

   ....

   ....

3. The hospital is very large (*use superlative*); Ann's room was on the third floor. ....

   ....

   ....

4. Ann was taking a cough syrup when Rita and James entered her room. ....

   ....

   ....

5. Turning to her friends, Ann exclaimed: "I am very glad to see you!" ....

   ....

   ....

6. Ann had a terrible cold and a very high fever. ....

   ....

7. She had a headache also, and her chest hurt (*use imp. of* **doler**). ....

   ....

8. Rita asked her friend whether she had slept well. ....

   ....

92

9. Ann replied that unfortunately she had coughed most of the night. ....

....

10. The doctor had prescribed some pills for her (*use indir. obj.*), and she felt somewhat better.

....

....

11. It didn't amuse her to be in bed, and she hoped to return to her classes as soon as possible.

....

....

12. Finally, James told her that it was necessary (*use imp. of* **haber que**) to be patient and to listen to

the doctor. ....

....

VI. Write answers to these questions, using complete sentences:

1. ¿Cómo se siente Ud. hoy?

....

2. ¿Tiene Ud. un resfriado?

....

3. ¿Le duele a Ud. alguna parte del cuerpo?

....

4. ¿A quién llamamos cuando estamos enfermos?

....

5. ¿Qué recetan los médicos para la tos?

....

6. ¿Adónde va mucha gente los domingos?

....

7. ¿Cuántas veces ha estado Ud. en el hospital este año?

....

8. ¿Qué les manda Ud. a sus amigos cuando están en el hospital?

   ....

   ....

Lección 17

I. Commands

A. Answer each question with negative and affirmative formal commands, following the model.

MODEL: ¿Hablo ahora?   *No, no hable Ud. ahora; hable más tarde.*

1. ¿Vuelvo ahora? ....

....

2. ¿Salgo ahora? ....

....

3. ¿Lo traemos ahora? ....

....

4. ¿Se lo decimos ahora? ....

....

B. Change each affirmative formal command to the negative:

1. Déselo Ud. a él. ....

2. Déjelos Ud. en la lista. ....

3. Pídaselo Ud. a Jaime. ....

4. Vaya Ud. en seguida. ....

C. Change each affirmative familiar command to the negative:

1. Elena, ve al almacén. ....

2. Lupe, busca la batidora. ....

3. Clara, dale la toalla. ....

4. Mario, ponte el sombrero. ....

II. Complete with the corresponding form of the verb:

1. (asistir)   Ana y Lupe quieren .... a misa.

2. (asistir)   Dígale Ud. a Carlos que .... al concierto.

3. (ver)   Queremos que Ud. .... el barrio.

4. (ir)   Le ruego a Ana que no .... a clase todavía.

5. (alquilar) Preferimos que ellos .... un estudio.

6. (dar)   Luis desea que yo .... un paseo con Marta.

7. (servir) ¿Quieres que nosotros .... el café ahora?

8. (venir) Dígales Ud. a los chicos que .... pronto.

9. (hacer) Sugiero que Uds. .... una cita con el gerente.

10. (tener) Pídales Ud. a todos que .... paciencia.

11. (conocer) ¿No quieres que Antonio .... a María?

12. (casarse) Sus familias prefieren que ellos .... el mes que viene.

III. Complete, making a subjunctive clause of the expression indicated in parentheses:

1. Quiero que Ud. (hablar con él). ....

    (pensarlo bien). ....

    (poner el disco). ....

    (oír la canción). ....

2. Desean que tú (sentarse aquí). ....

    (ver el cuarto). ....

    (pedirles algo). ....

    (saber nadar). ....

IV. Write in Spanish, noting the change in subject in the second sentence of the first two exercises:

1. Louis wishes to leave early. He wishes me to leave (wishes that I leave) early. ....

   ....

2. They prefer to stay several days. They prefer that we stay several days. ....

   ....

3. George suggests that I come with Mary. ....

   ....

4. ¿Do they suggest that we serve soft drinks? ....

   ....

96

5. Ask *(formal sing.)* him to lie down (ask of him that he lie down). ....

....

6. We beg you *(pl.)* to sit down. ....

....

7. I shall tell him to get up before six o'clock. ....

....

8. Tell *(formal sing.)* them that we prefer to wait here. ....

....

V. Write in Spanish:

1. Sylvia and Albert intend to get married next month. ....

....

2. They began to look for an apartment several weeks ago. ....

....

3. Since Albert doesn't earn much money, they prefer that the apartment be small and

   inexpensive. ....

....

4. Last week Albert saw a studio apartment that is furnished. ....

....

5. He wants Sylvia to go with him to see it as soon as possible. ....

....

....

6. Albert calls the manager; he (the latter) suggests that they come at 1:30. ....

....

....

7. Albert wants them to eat something before going to the apartment house. ....

....

....

8. But Sylvia asks: "Don't you prefer that we take a walk through the district to know it better?"

....

....

9. While they take the walk, they begin to talk about the appliances that they will need in their new home. ....

....

....

10. Sylvia says that among other things they will need a toaster, a percolator, and a vacuum cleaner. ....

....

11. Albert remembers that the apartment has a stove, a refrigerator, and a dishwasher. ....

....

....

12. The rent of the apartment is a bargain, and they decide to take it. ....

....

....

VI. Write answers to these questions, using complete sentences:

1. Cuando un joven y una joven se casan, ¿qué buscan generalmente?

....

2. ¿Hay muchos apartamentos amueblados en esta ciudad?

....

3. ¿Es caro o barato el alquiler de un apartamento en esta ciudad?

....

4. ¿Cuánto cuesta el alquiler de un estudio?

....

5. ¿Qué muebles se encuentran generalmente en un apartamento?

....

6. ¿Cuáles son algunos aparatos que se necesitan en la cocina?

....

....

7. ¿Qué otros aparatos se encuentran generalmente en un apartamento?

....

....

8. ¿Piensa Ud. casarse algún día?

....

Lección 18

I. Commands

A. Answer first with an affirmative formal command and then with a negative one, substituting object pronouns for noun objects, following the model.

MODEL: ¿Le doy a Carlos el boleto?   *Sí, déselo Ud. a él.*
No, no se lo dé Ud. a él.

1. ¿Busco las llaves?   ....

....

2. ¿Pago la cuenta?   ....

....

3. ¿Cruzo la calle?   ....

....

4. ¿Organizo el tráfico?   ....

....

5. ¿Empiezo la clase?   ....

....

6. ¿Saco las fotos?   ....

....

B. Change each affirmative familiar command to the negative:

1. Juan, llega a tiempo.   ....

2. Luis, juega con Jorge.   ....

3. Ana, entrégame el dinero.   ....

4. Mario, sigue adelante.   ....

5. Inés, almuerza con Juan.   ....

6. Elena, acércate a la mesa.   ....

II. Complete with the corresponding form of the present indicative or present subjunctive tense, as required:

1. (ir al centro) Creen que nosotros ....

       No creo que ellos ....

2. (jugar bien) Estoy seguro de que ella ....

       No están seguros de que yo ....

3. (tener buena suerte) Esperamos que Uds. ....

       ¿No crees que él ....?

4. (llegar tarde) Me sorprende que tú ....

       Dudamos que María ....

5. (oír los discos) Me alegro de que ellos ....

       Es lástima que tú no ....

6. (no poder esperar) Sentimos que Ud. ....

       No digo que nosotros ....

III. Complete the noun clause, using the corresponding form of the present perfect subjunctive tense:

1. Dudo que ellos lo traigan. ...... que ellos ....

2. Temen que Isabel lo diga. ...... que Isabel ....

3. Es lástima que Uds. lo vean. ...... que Uds. ....

4. No creo que ellas vuelvan. ...... que ellas ....

5. Sienten que yo lo sepa. ...... que yo ....

6. No estoy seguro de que tú vayas. ...... de que tú ....

IV. Change to an indirect command with *él*, preceded by «Yo no puedo», following the model.

MODEL: Envuélvalo Ud. *Yo no puedo, que lo envuelva él.*

1. Entréguelos Ud. ....

2. Acérquese Ud. ....

3. Lléveselas Ud. ....

4. Cuéntelos Ud. ....

V. Write three replies (two affirmative and one negative), substituting object pronouns for noun objects, following the model.

MODEL: ¿Compramos el carro?   *Sí, comprémoslo. Sí, vamos a comprarlo.*
No, no lo compremos.

1. ¿Sacamos otras fotos?   ....

    ....

2. ¿Seguimos el camino?   ....

    ....

3. ¿Hacemos el resumen?   ....

    ....

4. ¿Ponemos la televisión?   ....

    ....

VI. Write in Spanish:

1. Let's slow down (*two ways*).   ....

    ....

2. Let's sit down (*two ways*).   ....

    ....

3. Let's not go to class.   ....

4. Let's not pay the bill.   ....

5. May you (*pl.*) continue on!   ....

6. Have him put them (*m.*) on!   ....

7. Let (*pl.*) me drive.   ....

8. Perhaps they may get hurt.   ....

VII. Write in Spanish:

1. A famous economist will give a lecture in the university of a nearby city.   ....

    ....

2. The economics teacher (*m.*) asks his students to make a summary of the lecture.   ....

    ....

3. Three companions go with John in his car to the place where the lecture will be given. ....

....

....

4. There is so much traffic that Robert is afraid that they will not arrive on time. ....

....

5. John believes that perhaps there has been an accident. ....

....

6. Since they hear sirens, they know that the police will arrive soon. ....

....

7. When the patrol car approaches, Betty says that John ought to let it pass on the left. ....

....

....

8. Robert suggests that John not permit a taxi driver to go on ahead. ....

....

9. Finally John tells his friends that there are too many drivers. ....

....

10. He wants them to calm down and to let him drive. ....

....

11. Fortunately there haven't been injured persons; ambulances are not needed. ....

....

12. Finally Agnes exclaims that she doubts that a better driver than John can be found. ....

....

....

VIII. Write answers to these questions, using complete sentences:

1. ¿Le gusta a Ud. manejar un carro?

....

2. ¿Cuántos años tenía Ud. cuando aprendió a manejar?

....

3. ¿Tienen carros la mayor parte de los estudiantes de esta universidad?

   ....

4. ¿Modera Ud. la marcha cuando pasa un coche patrulla? ....

   ....

5. ¿Ha tenido Ud. o algún amigo suyo un accidente manejando un carro? ....

   ....

   ....

6. ¿Quiénes organizan el tráfico después de un accidente? ....

   ....

7. ¿A qué horas del día hay mucho tráfico en esta ciudad? ....

   ....

   ....

8. ¿Ha habido muchos accidentes de tráfico por aquí? ....

   ....

A. Find two or more verb cognates in the *Lectura*, Text, pp. 302–303, which illustrate the following principles: verbs ending in **-ar** = *-ate*; the English verb ends in *-e* or lacks the ending of the Spanish infinitive. Do not include verbs with additional variations in spelling.

....

....

....

....

B. Read each sentence carefully. If the statement is correct, rewrite it, beginning your sentence with "Sí." If the statement is incorrect, correct it, beginning your sentence with "No" and making the necessary changes:

1. Cabeza de Vaca fue el primer europeo que atravesó el continente norteamericano. ....

....

....

2. En 1540 Coronado encontró las Siete Ciudades de Cíbola. ....

....

3. La ciudad más antigua de los Estados Unidos fue fundada en la Florida en 1565. ....

....

....

4. El primer pueblo español en el valle del río Grande fue fundado por Juan de Oñate. ....

....

....

5. Cabrillo descubrió la Alta California en 1542. ....

....

6. Los españoles vinieron a América sólo para buscar riquezas. ....

....

....

7. Los misioneros fundaron pueblos, iglesias, misiones, escuelas y universidades. ....

....

....

8. Para visitar la hermosa misión de San Xavier del Bac hay que ir a San Antonio. ....

....

....

9. El padre Junípero Serra fundó una larga serie de misiones en California. ....

....

....

10. Debemos a los españoles todas las frutas que tenemos hoy día en las Américas. ....

....

....

11. Las naranjas, los limones, las aceitunas y las uvas son de España. ....

....

12. El maíz, el chocolate y el tabaco tuvieron su origen en Europa. ....

....

Lección 19

I. Complete with the infinitive, or the corresponding form of the present indicative or present subjunctive, as required:

1. (hacerse médico)   Es cierto que él ....

   Es urgente que yo ....

2. (saber conducir)   Es lástima que él no ....

   No es cierto que él no ....

3. (pensar en mí)   Es extraño que ella ....

   Es verdad que ella ....

4. (manejar el carro)   Será preciso que Ud. ....

   Es posible que ella ....

5. (traducir la carta)   Es mejor ....

   Es necesario que tú ....

6. (obtener el puesto)   Es difícil que Juan ....

   Es importante que Juan ....

II. Supply the relative pronouns (in some cases two or more are correct):

1. La señorita .... tradujo la carta...

2. Los ingenieros con .... hablamos...

3. Las mujeres .... nos llamaron...

4. El problema de .... me escribieron...

5. Las tarjetas .... recibimos...

6. El gerente de la empresa, ... reside en Puerto Rico,...

7. La hermana de Juan, ... está en Buenos Aires,...

8. La casa acerca de .... él me hablaba...

9. La chica al lado de .... yo estaba sentado...

10. El joven para .... escribí la recomendación...

11. Las hijas del profesor, ... están aquí de visita,...

12. Los estudiantes con .... cenamos...

13. La casa en .... residimos es de estilo español.

14. El padre de esa joven, ... acaba de llegar,...

15. Ellos volvieron tarde, ... me molestó mucho.

16. Miguel no nos trajo nada, ... nos sorprendió un poco.

III. Complete with the corresponding form of the present indicative or present subjunctive tense, as required:

1. Buscamos a la enfermera que (trabajar) .... los lunes.

2. Preferimos un médico que (hablar) .... español.

3. ¿Conocen Uds. a alguien que yo (poder) .... recomendar?

4. No conozco a nadie que (ser) .... tan trabajador como Miguel.

5. Nos interesa una secretaria que (saber) .... varias lenguas.

6. ¿Habló Ud. con los señores que (pensar) .... comprar este edificio?

7. No veo a nadie que (recordar) .... las palabras de la canción.

8. Buscan una persona que (querer) .... vivir en la isla.

9. No hay ninguna joven que (conocer) .... a la señora Ortega.

10. Tengo un amigo que (haber) .... sido gerente de esta empresa.

11. Necesitamos una persona que (haber) .... tenido varios años de experiencia.

12. En esa tienda nunca hallamos nada que nos (gustar) ....

IV. Supply the correct form of the verb in parentheses to express an action that started in the past and is still going on:

1. Hace seis meses que nosotros (estudiar) .... español.

2. Hace mucho tiempo que yo (pensar) .... estudiar medicina.

3. ¿Cuánto tiempo hace que Carlos (preparar) .... el artículo?

4. ¿Cuánto tiempo hace que Uds. (recibir) .... esa revista?

5. Miguel (trabajar) .... en esa compañía desde hace varias semanas.

6. Ana no (asistir) .... a clase desde hace un par de semanas.

V. Write the Spanish for:

1. We heard Betty sing. ....

2. I have heard (it said) that Agnes is here. ....

   ....

3. John almost went crazy. ....

4. "Thank you." "Don't mention it." ....

5. Charles became a doctor. ....

6. Ann became a nurse. ....

7. ¿Did Betty blush? ....

8. I hope they become calm. ....

VI. Write in Spanish:

1. Mr. Ruiz, who is the manager of a firm in Puerto Rico, has written a letter to the School of Agricultural Engineering. ....

   ....

2. Miss White, the secretary of the School, has just received the letter. ....

   ....

3. The manager needs a person who can work as an agent of the company on the island. ....

   ....

   ....

4. It is important that the person understand agricultural machinery and speak Spanish well. ......

   ....

   ....

5. On seeing Michael, a student of the School, Miss White calls him. ....

   ....

6. She tells him that she has heard (it said) that he is looking for work. ....

....

7. She shows Michael the letter and asks him whether the position interests him. ....

....

....

8. Michael replies that he is glad that she has thought of him. ....

....

....

9. He hopes that she will give him a good recommendation because he needs to find work soon.

....

....

10. Miss White promises to tell Mr. Ruiz that she doesn't know anyone who is more industrious than

Michael. ....

....

11. Mr. Ruiz is a friend whom Miss White met in Puerto Rico; she has known him for a couple of

years. ....

....

12. Miss White blushes when Michael translates for her some verses that Mr. Ruiz had written to her in

Spanish. ....

....

....

VII. Write answers to these questions, using complete sentences:

1. ¿Cuánto tiempo hace que Ud. asiste a esta universidad?

....

2. ¿Piensa Ud. hacerse médico o ingeniero?

....

3. ¿Le interesaría a Ud. obtener un puesto en Puerto Rico?

....

112

4. ¿Conoce Ud. a alguien que haya vivido en esa isla?

   ....

5. ¿Entiende Ud. algo de maquinaria agrícola?

   ....

6. ¿Es necesario que Ud. obtenga un puesto pronto?

   ....

7. ¿Es fácil encontrar trabajo hoy día?

   ....

8. Si Ud. necesita un puesto, ¿a quién pedirá que lo (la) recomiende?

   ....

   ....

Lección 20

I. Give the first person singular present indicative and present subjunctive tense of each infinitive:

	Present Indicative	*Present Subjunctive*
1. continuar	....	....
2. dirigir	....	....
3. enviar	....	....
4. escoger	....	....

II. The subjunctive in adverbial clauses

A. Complete with the corresponding form of the present subjunctive tense:

1. Entraremos en cuanto (llegar) .... el profesor.

    cuando (empezar) .... la conferencia.

2. Jugaré contigo a menos que Ana (querer) .... jugar.

    aunque (continuar) .... lloviendo.

3. Lo llamaré después que él (volver) .... del centro.

    antes de que ella (enviar) .... la ropa.

4. Dígaselo Ud. para que ella no (escoger) .... otro tema.

    antes de que ella (salir) .... de viaje.

B. Answer the questions affirmatively, following the pattern illustrated in the model.

MODEL: ¿Lo traerá Ud.?   *Sí, aunque Luis lo traiga también.*

1. ¿La enviará Ud.? ....

2. ¿Los escogerá Ud.? ....

3. ¿Continuará Ud. el viaje? ....

4. ¿Empezarán Uds. el plan? ....

5. ¿Harán Uds. la excursión? ....

6. ¿Obtendrá Ud. la beca? ....

C. Complete with the corresponding form of the present indicative or present subjunctive tense, as required:

1. El chico siempre me pide algo cuando me (ver) ....

2. Hable Ud. despacio para que nosotros lo (entender) ....

3. Después que Rita te (entregar) .... las fotos, tráemelas.

4. Iremos al aeropuerto, a menos que se (cancelar) .... el vuelo.

5. Ellos no podrán salir sin que nosotros los (oír) ....

6. Mi hermana me da la maleta para que yo la (facturar) ....

7. Yo siempre asisto a las fiestas en cuanto (llegar) .... a México.

8. No les dé Ud. nada hasta que ellos (sentarse) ....

III. Possessive pronouns

Answer the questions affirmatively, using a possessive pronoun for the italicized words:

1. ¿Trae Ud. *su pasaporte?* ....

2. ¿Halló Ud. *mis llaves?* ....

3. ¿Tiene Ud. *mi maleta?* ....

4. ¿Lleva Ud. *mis paquetes?* ....

5. ¿Ven Uds. *nuestro carro?* ....

6. ¿Es de plata *el anillo de Ana?* ....

7. ¿Vienen Uds. a *nuestro cuarto?* ....

8. ¿Compró Ud. *el boleto de Juan?* ....

IV. Use of the definite article as a demonstrative

A. Rewrite each sentence, substituting the corresponding definite article for the nouns before **de** and **que,** as in the models.

MODELS: Quiero ese mapa y el mapa de Ana.   *Quiero ese mapa y el de Ana.*
Esta blusa y la blusa que ella compró son bonitas.   *Esta blusa y la que ella compró son bonitas.*

1. Esta calle y la calle de Juárez son tranquilas.

....

116

2. ¿Le gusta a Ud. este lápiz o el lápiz que Isabel escogió?

....

3. Este coche y el coche de Juan son caros.

....

4. Me interesan esta canción y la canción que acabas de cantar.

....

B. Answer the following questions affirmatively, following the models:

MODELS: ¿Llegó ese joven ayer?   *Sí, es el que llegó ayer.*
         ¿Te gusta esta maleta?   *Sí, es la que me gusta.*

1. ¿Compró Luisa estos discos? ....

2. ¿Miraron Uds. esas fotos? ....

3. ¿Le gusta a Ud. aquel cuadro? ....

4. ¿Dejó Ud. esa revista allí? ....

C. Write the Spanish for:

1. John's scholarship and that of Helen are fantastic! ....

....

2. ¿Do you (*fam. sing.*) know the one (*f.*) in (**de**) the red dress? ....

....

3. Those who work hard get good positions. ....

....

4. ¿Don't you (*fam. sing.*) remember what they have said? ....

....

V. Uses of *pero* and *sino*

Complete with **pero** or **sino**, as required:

1. Vi una bandeja que me gusta, ... no pude comprarla.

2. Me dicen que no hicieron el viaje en coche, ... en tren.

3. Yo llamé a Marta, ... nadie contestó.

4. No quedan asientos en el vuelo de la tarde, ... en el de la mañana.

VI. Write in Spanish:

1. Albert and Sylvia, who have just gotten married, are going to spend their honeymoon in South America. ....

   ....

2. They had always wanted to visit the ancient city of Machu Picchu, near Cuzco. ....

   ....

   ....

3. The travel agency that they chose was that of Mr. Ponce, a friend of Albert's family. ....

   ....

   ....

4. Since Mr. Ponce didn't know Albert's wife, Albert introduced her to him. ....

   ....

5. Mr. Ponce said to her: "Pleased to know you (*formal f. sing.*);" then he invited them to sit down. ....

   ....

6. He tells them that there are direct flights to Panama, but not to Lima. ....

   ....

7. Sylvia then wants Mr. Ponce to inform them about the flight from Lima to Cuzco. ....

   ....

   ....

8. The date they have selected for (**para**) their departure is the fifteenth of August. ....

   ....

9. They would prefer a daytime flight, but Mr. Ponce informs them that there are no seats left on that flight. ....

   ....

10. They have to resign themselves to asking Mr. Ponce to put them on the waiting list. ....

    ....

11. They asked for round-trip tickets; Albert paid for them with a credit card. ....

    ....

12. On taking leave of Mr. Ponce, the latter informs them that they should not take more than two

suitcases, Albert's and hers. ....

....

....

VII. Write answers to these questions, using complete sentences:

1. Cuando uno quiere hacer un viaje, ¿dónde puede comprar los boletos?

....

....

2. ¿Hay varias agencias de viajes cerca de la universidad?

....

3. ¿Prefiere Ud. facturar sus maletas o llevarlas consigo cuando viaja?

....

....

4. ¿Prefiere Ud. comprar boletos sencillos o de ida y vuelta?

....

5. ¿Paga Ud. sus cuentas con tarjeta de crédito o con cheque personal?

....

6. ¿Adónde piensa Ud. ir en su próximo viaje?

....

7. ¿Le gustaría a Ud. continuar sus estudios en algún país extranjero?

....

....

8. ¿Qué necesita uno llevar para poder entrar en algunos países?

....

....

A. Find two or more words in the *Lectura,* Text, pp. 340-341, which illustrate the following principles: Spanish **-cia, -cio** = English *-ce;* **-ia, -io** = *-y;* **-ción** = *-tion;* **-oso** = *-ous.*

....

....

....

....

....

B. Identify briefly in Spanish—in a single phrase—the cities, states, regions, rivers, words, elements, date, and events to which the following statements refer:

1. Las partes de nuestro país que antes pertenecían al imperio español en América. ....

   ....

2. El estado cuyo nombre significa la tierra roja. ....

   ....

3. El estado que lleva el nombre de una isla que se menciona en una antigua novela española.

   ....

4. Dos ríos que tienen nombres españoles. ....

   ....

5. Las palabras españolas que han entrado en inglés en la forma de *canyon* y *palaver.* ....

   ....

6. Dos palabras que los españoles tomaron de las lenguas indígenas de América. ....

   ....

7. Dos elementos de las casas del suroeste de nuestro país que recuerdan la arquitectura

   española. ....

   ....

8. Dos elementos de la cultura española que se conservan todavía en el norte de Nuevo México y el sur de Colorado. ....

....

9. El año en que se proclamó el Estado Libre Asociado de Puerto Rico. ....

....

10. Dos ciudades importantes de la isla de Puerto Rico. ....

....

11. Uno de los fenómenos más significantes de los últimos treinta años. ....

....

12. La parte de nuestro país en que el aumento de la población de habla española ha sido más rápido. ....

....

Lección 21

I. Uses of the subjunctive mood

A. Rewrite each sentence, using the initial phrase given in parentheses, following the model. Use the **-ra** form of the imperfect subjunctive tense in the dependent clause of 1–4, and the **-se** form in 5–8.

MODEL: Es mejor que Uds. se vayan. (Fue mejor)   *Fue mejor que Uds. se fueran.*

1. Yo le aconsejo a Luis que les envíe la carta. (Yo le aconsejé) ....

....

2. José le dice que compare los precios. (José le dijo) ....

....

3. Será posible que ellos escojan otra marca. (Sería posible) ....

....

4. No hay nadie que comprenda eso. (No había) ....

....

5. Él sigue buscando una cámara que le guste. (Él seguía) ....

....

6. No es cierto que Jaime haga la excursión. (No fue cierto) ....

....

7. Te traigo el cheque para que lo cobres. (Te traje) ....

....

8. Quieren que nos encontremos enfrente de la casa de correos. (Querían) ....

....

B. Complete with the corresponding form of the present or imperfect subjunctive tense of the verb in parentheses, using the **-ra** form when the imperfect subjunctive tense is required:

1. Quiero que Alberto (buscar) .... otra maleta.

2. ¿Les aconsejaron a Uds. que (escoger) .... otra agencia?

3. Será preciso que ellos (irse) .... pronto.

4. Ellos se alegran de que nosotros no (tener) .... nada que hacer hoy.

5. Fue lástima que el novio de Silvia no (volver) .... de su viaje ayer.

6. Los novios buscaban un apartamento que (estar) .... cerca de la universidad.

7. Nosotros queríamos ver a Marta antes que ella (partir) .... para México.

8. No había nadie que (querer) .... asistir a la conferencia.

C. Complete with the corresponding form of the verb. When the imperfect or pluperfect subjunctive tense is required, use the **-ra** form:

1. Le rogué a Inés que (estar) .... lista a las seis.

2. Le dimos cien dólares para que él (poder) .... comprar el boleto.

3. Sería mejor que mis tíos (haber) .... comprado su casa.

4. No había nadie que (haber) .... sido más trabajador que Miguel.

5. ¡Cuánto me alegro de que José (haber) .... conseguido el puesto!

6. Yo le aconsejo a Ud. que no (preocuparse) .... por eso.

7. Le pediremos al agente que nos (poner) .... en la lista de espera.

8. Mi hermana me pidió que (comprar) .... otro rollo de película.

9. Saldremos en cuanto Lola (hacer) .... las maletas.

10. No pudimos visitar a Juan antes de que él (ir) .... al hospital.

11. A José le gustaría que nosotros (ver) .... sus transparencias.

12. Es lástima que Uds. no (asistir) .... a la conferencia ayer.

II. Conditional sentences

A. Complete with the corresponding form of the verb. When the imperfect subjunctive tense is required, use the **-ra** form.

1. Si nosotros (hacer) .... las reservas pronto, podremos hacer el viaje.

2. Ella sacaría muchas fotos, si (llevar) .... una cámara.

3. Yo le haría algunas preguntas si (encontrarse) .... con él.

4. Yo llevaría un paraguas si (estar) .... lloviendo ahora.

5. Si yo (haber) .... sabido que Luis estaba aquí, lo habría llamado.

6. Si Ud. (poder) .... mandarnos el artículo, se lo agradeceríamos mucho.

124

B. Form new conditional sentences, following the model:

MODEL: Yo lo haría, pero no tengo tiempo.   *Si yo tuviera tiempo, lo haría.*

1. Luis le enviaría una tarjeta, pero no sabe su dirección.

    ....

2. Iríamos contigo, pero no tenemos boletos.

    ....

3. Alquilaríamos el apartamento, pero no está amueblado.

    ....

4. Yo me pondría el abrigo, pero no hace frío.

    ....

5. Yo le daría algunos consejos, pero él no me consulta.

    ....

6. Yo leería el libro, pero no vale la pena leerlo.

    ....

III. Write the Spanish for:

1. Of course! (*two ways*)   ....

    ....

2. We don't mean that.   ....

3. It wouldn't be worthwhile.   ....

4. We are very sorry.   ....

5. She asked me a question.   ....

6. I'll be ready at any hour.   ....

7. We'll be there without fail.   ....

8. I have nothing to do today.   ....

IV. Write in Spanish:

1. Mr. Ponce has just informed Albert and Sylvia that he has had no problems with their trip.

....

....

2. They have been lucky; all the necessary reservations have been made. ....

....

....

3. On leaving the travel agency, they ran across Joseph Soto, a good friend of theirs. ....

....

....

4. Joseph is a Cuban engineer who knows South America very well. ....

....

....

5. They stopped to talk with him; they had the opportunity to ask him a few questions. ....

....

....

6. When they informed him about their plans, he invited them to his home to see his slides.

....

....

7. They were somewhat worried about the clothing they should take. ....

....

....

8. Sylvia also told Joseph that her father wanted them to look for a new camera. ....

....

....

9. Her father had said that he would buy it for them if they found (should find) one that they

liked. ....

....

....

10. If they brought back good slides, they would have unforgettable memories of their trip. ....

....

....

11. Since they haven't looked for the camera yet, Joseph said that he would accompany them (in order)

to compare various makes. ....

....

....

12. Sylvia suggested that they meet in front of the post office on the following day. ....

....

....

V. Write answers to these questions, using complete sentences:

1. Si Ud. pudiera hacer un viaje por nuestro país este verano, ¿qué estados visitaría?

....

....

2. ¿Haría Ud. el viaje en coche, en tren o en avión?

....

3. ¿Tendría Ud. que comprar una maleta si tuviera que salir de viaje pronto?

....

....

4. ¿Ha tenido Ud. la oportunidad de viajar con un grupo de amigos?

....

5. Si Ud. necesitara más dinero durante su viaje, ¿a quién se lo pediría?

....

....

6. ¿A quiénes escribiría Ud. cartas o tarjetas durante el viaje?

....

....

7. ¿Saca Ud. muchas fotografías cuando viaja?

....

8. ¿Prefiere Ud. llevar un paraguas o un impermeable cuando viaja?

....

Lección 22

I. Commands

A. Change to affirmative and negative plural formal commands:

1. Uds. lo hacen.   ....

2. Uds. lo envían.   ....

3. Uds. se van.   ....

B. Change to affirmative and negative singular familiar commands:

1. Tú lo consigues.   ....

2. Tú la construyes.   ....

3. Tú te sientas.   ....

C. Change to affirmative and negative plural familiar commands:

1. Vete (tú).   ....

2. Dilo (tú).   ....

3. Lávate (tú).   ....

II. Rewrite, changing the active verb to the passive voice:

1. Un amigo mío recibió estos libros.

....

2. El profesor preparó los exámenes anoche.

....

3. El gerente recomendó a Jorge para el puesto.

....

4. Una compañía mexicana construyó estos edificios.

....

5. Tomás sacó esas fotos el verano pasado.

....

6. José facturó las maletas ayer.

....

III. Rewrite the following sentences, substituting the phrase in parentheses for the italicized words:

1. *Me gustaría* viajar por España. (Yo quisiera)

....

2. *Debemos* detenernos aquí. (Debiéramos)

....

3. *¡Cuánto me alegro de que* él venga! (¡Ojalá que)

....

4. *Quizás* ellos no se reúnan mañana. (Tal vez)

....

5. *¡Ojalá que* nos veamos en la reunión! (Yo espero que)

....

6. *Yo quiero* almorzar en aquel restaurante. (Yo quisiera)

....

IV. Complete with the corresponding form of the imperfect subjunctive tense of *querer* and *deber*, forming polite or softened statements:

1. (deber)   Silvia .... ponerse un suéter, porque hace frío.

2. (deber)   Tú .... arreglar el carro antes de salir de viaje.

3. (querer)   Yo .... felicitar a Miguel.

4. (querer)   Nosotros .... que Miguel llegara a ser el gerente.

V. Write the Spanish for:

1. We would like to see him.   ....

2. We see each other often.   ....

3. Would that Michael were here!   ....

130

4. He has been very successful. ....

5. May you (*pl.*) become rich! ....

6. It is time to go to class. ....

7. Don't fail (*pl.*) to sign it (*f.*) ....

8. Let's get together tomorrow. ....

VI. Uses of *para* and *por*

Complete with **para** or **por,** as required:

1. ¿Qué planes tienen Uds. .... el verano? 2. Pensamos viajar .... Suramérica.

3. Estaremos allí .... celebrar mi cumpleaños. 4. No me gusta estudiar .... la

mañana. 5. Espero que Ud. pueda regresar .... las seis. 6. Ellos han preguntado

.... la novia de Carlos. 7. Los boletos son .... el partido del viernes.

8. Muchas gracias .... la carta de recomendación. 9. ¿Vas a volver ....

continuar tus estudios aquí? 10. .... fin Jorge anuncia que es hora de irse. 11. Vamos

a reunirnos pasado mañana .... cenar. 12. La carta fue firmada .... María.

13. Tenemos que ir .... las chicas. 14. ¡No se preocupen Uds. .... lo que

digan! 15. Mi abuelo me dará el dinero .... comprar el traje. 16. Ella pagó treinta

dólares .... los guantes. 17. ¿Tienes tiempo .... dar un paseo conmigo?

18. Es agradable pasearse .... aquí. 19. .... ejemplo, podríamos ir al parque.

20. Prepárense Uds. .... salir en seguida.

VII. Write in Spanish, using peninsular forms of address in sentence 10:

1. Several companions are having lunch in a restaurant that was recommended to them by

   Michael. ....

   ....

2. They have gathered to take leave of one another before leaving the university. ....

   ....

   ....

3. Unfortunately Michael had another commitment and was unable to attend the gathering. ....

....

....

4. He is very busy preparing (himself) for his departure for Puerto Rico. ....

....

5. His friends are glad that he has obtained a good position there, and they would like to congratulate

him. ....

....

6. After spending the summer on the coast, Betty will return in the fall (in order) to continue her

studies. ....

....

7. George, one of the young men, has a (the) master's degree in business administration. ....

....

....

8. He is Spanish, and his parents have begged him to return to Spain. ....

....

9. His father would like his son to work there as manager of his company. ....

....

....

10. George, who uses peninsular forms, tells his friends: "Don't fail (*fam. pl.*) to visit me when you

travel to Spain." ....

....

11. His friends hope that he will be very successful and that he will be able to return to the United

States often. ....

....

12. While they were having coffee, the waiter brought a cake on which Michael had written: "Let's not

say goodbye, but until later." ....

....

....

VIII. Write answers to these questions, using complete sentences:

1. ¿En qué mes termina Ud. sus exámenes este año?

   ....

   ....

2. ¿Piensa Ud. continuar sus estudios aquí en el otoño?

   ....

   ....

3. ¿Quién le aconsejó a Ud. que estudiara español?

   ....

   ....

4. ¿Qué formas de los verbos emplea Ud., las peninsulares o las que se emplean en Hispanoamérica?

   ....

   ....

5. Si Ud. tuviera la oportunidad, ¿qué otras lenguas estudiaría?

   ....

   ....

6. ¿Qué planes tiene Ud. para el verano?

   ....

   ....

7. ¿Qué hizo Ud. el verano pasado?

   ....

   ....

8. ¿Tendrá Ud. que trabajar para ganar dinero este verano?

   ....

   ....

Laboratory Manual

Lección 1

All exercises are to be done in conjunction with the tape for Lección 1, Reel 1.

I. Dialogue exercises

A. The speaker will read four unfinished sentences based on the first dialogue. Each unfinished sentence will be read twice. Select the word or phrase that best completes the meaning of the sentence and write it next to the corresponding number.

un poco   los alumnos   el español   la lección

1. ....*los alumnos*.................   3. ....*un poco*.......................

2. ....*la lección*.....................   4. ....*el español*...................

B. The speaker will read six statements based on the second dialogue. Each statement will be read twice. Circle **sí** if the statement is correct; circle **no** if it is incorrect.

1. sí (no)   4. (sí) no

2. (sí) no   5. sí (no)

3. sí (no)   6. sí (no)

II. Pronunciation drills

A. Listen carefully to the following words. Each word will be read twice. Each word will contain either an English long *a* or a Spanish **e** sound. For each word circle the letter representing the sound that you hear.

1. English (*a*)   Spanish **e**   4. English (*a*)   Spanish **e**

2. English *a*   Spanish (**e**)   5. English *a*   Spanish (**e**)

3. English *a*   Spanish (**e**)   6. English *a*   Spanish (**e**)   7. *English*

B. Listen carefully to the following words. Each word will be read twice. Each word will contain either an English long *o* or a Spanish **o** sound. For each word circle the letter representing the sound that you hear.

1. English (*o*)   Spanish **o**   4. English *o*   Spanish (**o**)

2. English *o*   Spanish (**o**)   5. English *o*   Spanish (**o**)

3. English (*o*)   Spanish **o**   6. English *o*   Spanish **o**

C. When you hear the number, read the corresponding phrase or sentence aloud, paying special attention to the linking of vowels between words and to the linking of the final consonant of a word to the initial vowel of a following word. Then listen as the speaker reads the phrase or sentence, and repeat.

1. la clase de español

2. la lección de inglés

3. con los alumnos

4. los Estados Unidos

5. ¿Habla usted italiano?

6. No estudio alemán.

III. Structure drills. Listening and writing drills

A. The speaker will read eight words. Each word will be read twice. Write each word in the space provided and then supply the corresponding definite article. After you have finished writing all the words, make each one plural, following the model.*

MODEL: alumna
       la alumna   *las alumnas* (plural)

1. el habla, usted habla, tu hablas, yo hablo

2. prepara, preparamos, prepara, preparas

3. estudia, estudia, estudian, estudiamos

4. pronuncian, pronunciamos, pronuncia, pronuncias

5.

6.

7.

8.

B. Dictation

Get ready to write the sentences you will hear. Each sentence will be read twice. After the first reading, try to write all that you have heard; after the second reading, fill in what you have missed.

1.

2.

3.

4.

5.

*NOTE TO STUDENT: Remember to stop the tape or cassette after writing all the entries the first time. This applies to all exercises in which transformations are required.

NAME ....

SECTION ....

DATE ....

All exercises are to be done in conjunction with the tape for Lección 2, Reel 2.

I. Dialogue exercises

A. The speaker will read six statements based on the first dialogue. Each statement will be read twice. Circle **sí** if the statement is correct; circle **no** if it is incorrect.

1. sí   no   4. sí   no

2. sí   no   5. sí   no

3. sí   no   6. sí   no

B. The speaker will read six unfinished sentences based on the second dialogue. Each unfinished sentence will be read twice. Select the word or phrase that best completes the meaning of the sentence and write it next to the corresponding number.

las paredes	verde	buenas
la cafetería	grande	bonita

1. ....   4. ....

2. ....   5. ....

3. ....   6. ....

II. Pronunciation drills

A. Listen carefully to the following words. Each word will be read twice. Each word will contain either a **t** or a **d** sound. For each word, circle the letter representing the sound (**t** or **d**) that you hear

1. t   d   5. t   d

2. t   d   6. t   d

3. t   d   7. t   d

4. t   d   8. t   d

B. Listen carefully to the following words and phrases. Each will be read twice. Each word or phrase will contain one of the two sounds of Spanish **d**: either the sound like English *d* or the sound like English *th* in *this*. For each word or phrase, circle the letter representing the sound (*d* or *th* in *this*) that you hear.

1. d   th (in *this*)   5. d   th (in *this*)

2. d   th (in *this*)   6. d   th (in *this*)

3. d   th (in *this*)   7. d   th (in *this*)

4. d   th (in *this*)   8. d   th (in *this*)

III. Structure drills. Listening and writing drills

A. The speaker will read six incomplete sentences. Each incomplete sentence will be read twice. Each lacks a verb. Select the verb form that best completes the meaning of the sentence and write it next to the corresponding number.

es   somos   son
tienen   tengo   tenemos

1. ....   4. ....

2. ....   5. ....

3. ....   6. ....

B. Dictation

Get ready to write the sentences you will hear. Each sentence will be read twice. After the first reading, try to write all that you have heard; after the second reading, fill in what you have missed.

1. ....

2. ....

3. ....

4. ....

5. ....

All exercises are to be done in conjunction with the tape for Lección 3, Reel 2.

I. Dialogue exercises

A. The speaker will read five unfinished sentences based on the first dialogue. Each unfinished sentence will be read twice. For each one, select the phrase that best completes the sentence and circle the letter before it.

1. a. los ejercicios

   b. en la pizarra

   c. una carta

2. a. en un apartamento

   b. en una residencia

   c. en una casa

3. a. las dos de la tarde

   b. las siete y veinte

   c. las diez de la noche

4. a. a las doce

   b. por la tarde

   c. a las ocho y media

5. a. tomar un refresco

   b. tomar el almuerzo

   c. tomar el desayuno

B. The speaker will read five statements based on the second dialogue. Each statement will be read twice. Circle **sí** if the statement is correct; circle **no** if it is incorrect.

1. sí   no

2. sí   no

3. sí   no

4. sí   no

5. sí   no

II. Pronunciation drills

A. Listen carefully to the following words and phrases. Each will be read twice. Each word or phrase will contain one or more of the two sounds of Spanish **b.** For each word or phrase, circle the letter **b** or **v** if it sounds like English *b.*

1. bastante
2. verde
3. habla
4. la verdad

5. vivimos
6. universidad
7. bien
8. voy

9. no voy
10. yo bebo

B. When you hear the number, read the corresponding numeral aloud. Then listen as the speaker reads the numeral and repeat.

1. dieciséis
2. diecisiete
3. dieciocho
4. diecinueve

5. veinte
6. veintiuno
7. veintidós
8. veintitrés

9. treinta y uno
10. treinta y dos

III. Structure drills. Listening and writing drills

A. You will hear four statements referring to things one does at different times of the day. Each statement will be followed by the question *¿Qué hora es?* Select the probable answer to each question by circling the letter before it. Each statement and question will be read twice.

1. a. Son las seis de la mañana.

   b. Son las tres de la tarde.

   c. Son las diez de la noche.

2. a. Son las once de la noche.

   b. Son las cinco de la mañana.

   c. Son las ocho y media de la mañana.

3. a. Es la una de la mañana.

   b. Son las siete y media de la mañana.

   c. Son las dos de la tarde.

4. a. Son las nueve de la mañana.

   b. Son las cinco de la tarde.

   c. Son las doce y cuarto.

B. Dictation

Get ready to write the sentences you will hear. Each sentence will be read twice. After the first reading, try to write all that you have heard; after the second reading, fill in what you have missed.

1. ....

2. ....

3. ....

4. ....

5. ....

Lección 4

All exercises are to be done in conjunction with the tape for Lección 4, Reel 3.

I. Dialogue exercises

A. The speaker will read six unfinished sentences based on the first dialogue. Each unfinished sentence will be read twice. For each one, select the word that best completes the meaning of the sentence and write it next to the corresponding number.

nuevas	vieja	españolas
extranjeros	actualidad	diccionario

1. .... 4. ....

2. .... 5. ....

3. .... 6. ....

B. The speaker will read six statements based on the second dialogue. Each statement will be read twice. Circle **sí** if the statement is correct; circle **no** if it is incorrect.

1. sí   no   4. sí   no

2. sí   no   5. sí   no

3. sí   no   6. sí   no

II. Pronunciation drills

A. Listen carefully to the following words. Each word will be read twice. Each word will contain one of the three sounds of Spanish **g.** For each word circle the letter **g** if the sound you hear is that of English *g* in *go.*

1. g   4. g   7. g

2. g   5. g   8. g

3. g   6. g

B. When you hear the number, read the corresponding word or phrase aloud. Then listen as the speaker reads the word or phrase and repeat it.

1. ahora   4. lejos   7. viejo

2. Jorge   5. él habla   8. por ejemplo

3. hispánico   6. argentino

III. Structure drills. Listening and writing drills

A. Get ready to write the sentences you will hear. The speaker will read two short sentences for each entry. Write them. Each entry will be read twice. After you have finished writing all the entries, combine both sentences using a possessive adjective, as in the following model.

MODEL: Tengo un amigo. Es cubano.
        Tengo un amigo. Es cubano.
        Mi amigo es cubano. (combined form)

1. ....

....

2. ....

....

3. ....

....

4. ....

....

5. ....

....

6. ....

....

B. The speaker will read six familiar singular commands. Each command will be read twice. Write the commands as you hear them. After you have finished, change affirmative commands to negative commands, and negative commands to affirmative ones.

1. ....

....

2. ....

....

3. ....

....

4. ....

....

5. ....

....

6. ....

....

Lección 5

All exercises are to be done in conjunction with the tape for Lección 5, Reel 3.

I. Dialogue exercises

A. The speaker will read five unfinished sentences based on the first dialogue. Each unfinished sentence will be read twice. For each one, select the phrase that best completes the meaning of the sentence and circle the letter before it.

1. a. inglés

   b. mexicano

   c. suramericano

2. a. del Uruguay

   b. de Buenos Aires

   c. de España

3. a. a la Argentina

   b. a la universidad

   c. a su país

4. a. en México

   b. en Montevideo

   c. por aquí

5. a. a las cinco

   b. a las ocho

   c. mañana

B. The speaker will now read five unfinished sentences based on the second dialogue. Each unfinished sentence will be read twice. For each one, select the phrase that best completes the meaning of the sentence and circle the letter before it.

1. a. a Diana

   b. a Tomás

   c. a sus padres

2. a. está ocupada

   b. está un poco enferma

   c. necesita descansar

3. a. largo

   b. corto

   c. interesante

4. a. en la librería

   b. en el laboratorio

   c. en la oficina

5. a. no está muy bien hoy

   b. después viene Tomás

   c. después vienen sus hermanas

II. Pronunciation drills

A. Listen carefully to the following words. Each word will be read twice. Each word will contain an **e**, **ie**, or **ei** (**ey**) sound. For each word circle the vowel or the vowel combination that you hear.

1. e	ie	ei	5. e	ie	ei	9. e	ie	ei
2. e	ie	ei	6. e	ie	ei	10. e	ie	ei
3. e	ie	ei	7. e	ie	ei
4. e	ie	ei	8. e	ie	ei

B. Listen carefully to the following words. Each word will be read twice. Each word will contain one of the sounds of Spanish **r**: either the simple **r** or the strongly trilled **r** (**rr**). For each word circle the letter representing the sound (simple **r** or trilled **rr**) that you hear.

1. r	rr	5. r	rr	9. r	rr
2. r	rr	6. r	rr	10. r	rr
3. r	rr	7. r	rr
4. r	rr	8. r	rr

III. Structure drills. Listening and writing drills

A. The speaker will read six incomplete sentences. Each incomplete sentence will be read twice. Each sentence lacks a verb. For each sentence, select the verb form that best completes the meaning of the sentence and write it next to the corresponding number.

está	estamos	están
soy	es	son

1. .... 4. ....

2. .... 5. ....

3. .... 6. ....

B. Dictation

Get ready to write the sentences you will hear. Each sentence will be read twice. After the first reading, try to write all that you have heard; after the second reading, fill in what you have missed.

1. ....

2. ....

3. ....

4. ....

5. ....

150

NAME ....

SECTION ....

DATE ....

All exercises are to be done in conjunction with the tape for Lección 6, Reel 4.

I. Dialogue exercises

A. The speaker will read five statements based on the first dialogue. Each statement will be read twice. Circle **sí** if the statement is correct; circle **no** if it is incorrect.

1. sí   no   4. sí   no

2. sí   no   5. sí   no

3. sí   no

B. The speaker will now read five statements based on the second dialogue. Each statement will be read twice. Circle **sí** if the statement is correct; circle **no** if it is incorrect.

1. sí   no   4. sí   no

2. sí   no   5. sí   no

3. sí   no

II. Pronunciation drills

A. Listen carefully to the following sentences. Each sentence will be read twice. Each sentence will contain the sound of Spanish **ch, y, ll,** or **ñ.** For each sentence, circle the letter representing the sound that you hear.

1. ch   y   ll   ñ   6. ch   y   ll   ñ

2. ch   y   ll   ñ   7. ch   y   ll   ñ

3. ch   y   ll   ñ   8. ch   y   ll   ñ

4. ch   y   ll   ñ   9. ch   y   ll   ñ

5. ch   y   ll   ñ   10. ch   y   ll   ñ

B. When you hear the number, read the corresponding sentence aloud, paying special attention to the linking of vowels between words and to the linking of the final consonant of a word to the initial vowel of a following word. Then listen as the speaker reads the sentence and repeat.

1. Su hermana vive en la Argentina.

2. Tomás lo invita a cenar.

3. Las va a traer a tomar algo.

4. ¿Conoce usted al señor Ortega?

5. ¿Busca usted a su amigo?

III. Structure drills. Listening and writing drills

A. Get ready to write the sentences you will hear. Each sentence will be read twice. Write each sentence. After you have finished, rewrite each sentence, substituting the direct object pronoun for the direct object, as in the model.

MODEL: Él compra las revistas mexicanas.
Él compra las revistas mexicanas. Él las compra.

1. ....

....

2. ....

....

3. ....

....

4. ....

....

5. ....

....

6. ....

....

B. Get ready to write the sentences you will hear. Each sentence will be read twice. After the first reading, try to write all that you have heard; after the second reading, fill in what you have missed.

1. ....

2. ....

3. ....

4. ....

5. ....

All exercises are to be done in conjunction with the tape for *Lección 7, Reel 4.*

I. Dialogue exercises

A. The speaker will ask five questions based on the first dialogue. Indicate the correct answer to each question by circling the letter before it.

1. a. en Buenos Aires

   b. en España

   c. en San Diego

2. a. en Montevideo

   b. en Tijuana

   c. en San Diego

3. a. Jorge

   b. Diana

   c. Silvia

4. a. charlar con su amiga

   b. visitar la ciudad

   c. comprar varias cosas

5. a. a las once

   b. a las nueve y media

   c. a la una de la tarde

B. The speaker will ask five questions based on the second dialogue. Indicate the correct answer to each question by circling the letter before it.

1. a. a la oficina

   b. al banco

   c. al centro

2. a. unos zapatos

   b. unos vestidos

   c. unas blusas

3. a. talla catorce

   b. talla ocho

   c. talla diez

4. a. el vestido blanco

   b. el vestido azul

   c. el vestido rojo

5. a. unas faldas

   b. unos pantalones

   c. una bolsa y un sombrero

II. Pronunciation drill

The speaker will read twelve words or phrases containing the diphthong sounds **ai**, **oi**, **ua**, and **au**, studied in this lesson. Each word or phrase will be read twice. For each word or phrase, circle the diphthong that you hear.

1. ai	oi	ua	au	7. ai	oi	ua	au
2. ai	oi	ua	au	8. ai	oi	ua	au
3. ai	oi	ua	au	9. ai	oi	ua	au
4. ai	oi	ua	au	10. ai	oi	ua	au
5. ai	oi	ua	au	11. ai	oi	ua	au
6. ai	oi	ua	au	12. ai	oi	ua	au

III. Structure drills. Listening and writing drills

A. The speaker will read four pairs of sentences. Each pair of sentences will be read twice. Write each pair. After you have finished, write a new sentence making a comparison based on each pair of sentences. Then write another sentence expressing the superlative degree, as in the model.

MODEL: Ana es bonita. Laura es más bonita.
Ana es bonita. Laura es más bonita.
Laura es más bonita que Ana. (comparison)
Laura es la más bonita de todas. (superlative)

1. ....

....

2. ....

....

3. ....

....

4. ....

....

B. Dictation

Get ready to write the sentences you will hear. Each sentence will be read twice. After the first reading, try to write all that you have heard; after the second reading, fill in what you have missed.

1. ....

2. ....

3. ....

4. ....

5. ....

Lección 8

All exercises are to be done in conjunction with the tape for Lección 8, Reel 5.

I. Dialogue exercise

The speaker will read ten statements based on the two dialogues. Each statement will be read twice. Circle **sí** if the statement is correct; circle **no** if it is incorrect.

1. sí   no   6. sí   no

2. sí   no   7. sí   no

3. sí   no   8. sí   no

4. sí   no   9. sí   no

5. sí   no   10. sí   no

II. Pronunciation drills

A. The sounds of **m** and **n**

When you hear the number, read the corresponding word or phrase aloud. Then listen as the speaker reads the word or phrase and repeat.

1. con papá   5. inglés

2. ingeniería   6. un vestido

3. un viaje   7. con Jorge

4. en casa   8. un poco

B. The sounds of the diphthongs **eu, ue**

The speaker will read eight words or phrases. Each word or phrase will contain the diphthong **eu** or **ue.** For each one, circle the diphthong you hear.

1. eu   ue   5. eu   ue

2. eu   ue   6. eu   ue

3. eu   ue   7. eu   ue

4. eu   ue   8. eu   ue

III. Structure drills. Listening and writing drills

A. Verb forms and subject pronouns

The speaker will read eight verb forms. Each form will be read twice. Write each one. After you have finished, write the corresponding plural form, as in the model.

MODEL: yo como   *yo como*   *nosotros comemos*

1. ....

2. ....

3. ....

4. ....

5. ....

6. ....

7. ....

8. ....

B. Dictation

Get ready to write the sentences you will hear. Each sentence will be read twice. After the first reading, try to write all that you have heard; after the second reading, fill in what you have missed.

1. ....

2. ....

3. ....

4. ....

5. ....

Lección 9

All exercises are to be done in conjunction with the tape for Lección 9, Reel 5.

I. Dialogue exercise

The speaker will ask ten questions based on the dialogue. Indicate the correct answer to each question by circling the letter before it.

1. a. en el mes de febrero

   b. en el mes de diciembre

   c. en el mes de agosto

2. a. en la calle

   b. en un cine

   c. en una cafetería

3. a. la semana pasada

   b. un domingo por la noche

   c. anoche

4. a. sí, Lola contestó

   b. sí, alguien contestó

   c. no, nadie contestó

5. a. a un primo de Lola

   b. a Lola

   c. a Jorge

6. a. Lola y Sara Cabral

   b. los primos de Lola

   c. unos amigos de Jorge

7. a. en España

   b. en la Argentina

   c. en Norteamérica

8. a. Sara Cabral

   b. Julio Iglesias

   c. Jorge Ibarra

9. a. los tíos de Lola

   b. los hermanos de Jorge

   c. Lola y Sara Cabral

10. a. porque Lola está ocupada

    b. porque ya es tarde

    c. porque ya comienza la película

II. Pronunciation drills

A. The sounds of Spanish s

Listen carefully to the following words and phrases. Each word or phrase will be read twice. Each will contain one of the two sounds of Spanish s: either the sound like English s in *sent* or the sound like English s in *rose*. For each word or phrase, circle the type of s you hear, that is, the s sound in *sent*, or the s sound in *rose*.

1. s (in *sent*)   s (in *rose*)   5. s (in *sent*)   s (in *rose*)

2. s (in *sent*)   s (in *rose*)   6. s (in *sent*)   s (in *rose*)

3. s (in *sent*)   s (in *rose*)   7. s (in *sent*)   s (in *rose*)

4. s (in *sent*)   s (in *rose*)   8. s (in *sent*)   s (in *rose*)

B. Linking

When you hear the number, read the corresponding sentence aloud, paying special attention to the linking of vowels between words and to the linking of the final consonant of a word to the initial vowel of a following word. Then listen as the speaker reads the sentence and repeat.

1. Encuentro a mi amiga.

2. Nunca te escribí.

3. Dio un concierto allí.

4. Escriben el anuncio.

5. Va a ser interesante.

6. ¿Qué estudian ellos?

7. ¿Vive ella en Los Ángeles?

8. ¿Quieres mucho o poco?

III. Structure drills. Listening and writing drills

A. You will hear five sentences. Each sentence will be read twice. Write them. Then, for each negative sentence, write an affirmative one, and for each affirmative sentence, write a negative one, as in the model.

MODEL: Quiero algo.   *Quiero algo. No quiero nada.*

1. ....

....

2. ....

....

3. ....

....

4. ....

....

5. ....

....

B. Dictation

Get ready to write the sentences you will hear. Each sentence will be read twice. After the first reading, try to write all that you have heard; after the second reading, fill in what you have missed.

1. ....

2. ....

3. ....

4. ....

5. ....

Lección 10

All exercises are to be done in conjunction with the tape for Lección 10, Reel 6.

I. Dialogue exercise

The speaker will read ten unfinished sentences based on the dialogue. Each unfinished sentence will be read twice. For each one, select the phrase that best completes the sentence and circle the letter before it.

1. a. tomaban el desayuno

   b. iban camino de Los Ángeles

   c. esperaban al profesor

2. a. sus estudios

   b. las elecciones

   c. su niñez

3. a. la primavera aquí

   b. el invierno aquí

   c. el otoño aquí

4. a. tenía varias casas

   b. tenía una librería

   c. tenía ganado

5. a. a Los Ángeles

   b. a este país

   c. a la universidad

6. a. en el campo

   b. en Cuba

   c. en Los Ángeles

7. a. del Caribe

   b. hermoso

   c. de la frontera

8. a. inglés

   b. español

   c. italiano

9. a. iba al cine

   b. iba a la playa

   c. salía de excursión

10. a. una playa preciosa

    b. una tormenta horrible

    c. unas tiendas interesantes

II. Pronunciation drills

A. Spanish **j**, and **g** before **e**, **i**

When you hear the number, read the corresponding word aloud. Then listen as the speaker reads the word and repeat.

1. viejo	3. trabajar	5. Jorge	7. Los Ángeles
2. lejos	4. generalmente	6. gente	8. argentino

B. Spanish **x**

Listen carefully to the following words. Each word will be read twice. Each contains one of the two sounds of Spanish **x**. Circle the letter representing the sound that you hear.

1. s gs	4. s gs	7. s gs
2. s gs	5. s gs	8. s gs
3. s gs	6. s gs	

III. Structure drills. Listening and writing drills

A. The speaker will read eight verb forms. Each form will be read twice. Write each one. When you have finished writing all the verb forms, change the singular forms to the corresponding plural forms and the plural forms to the corresponding singular ones.

1. ....

2. ....

3. ....

4. ....

5. ....

6. ....

7. ....

8. ....

B. Dictation

Get ready to write the sentences you will hear. Each sentence will be read twice. After the first reading, try to write all that you have heard; after the second reading, fill in what you have missed.

1. ....

2. ....

3. ....

4. ....

5. ....

Lección 11

All exercises are to be done in conjunction with the tape for Lección 11, Reel 6.

I. Dialogue exercise

The speaker will read ten statements based on the dialogue. Each statement will be read twice. Circle **sí** if the statement is correct; circle **no** if it is incorrect.

1. sí   no   6. sí   no

2. sí   no   7. sí   no

3. sí   no   8. sí   no

4. sí   no   9. sí   no

5. sí   no   10. sí   no

II. Pronunciation exercise

The pronunciation of **y**, *and*

When you hear the number, read the corresponding phrase or sentence aloud. Then listen as the speaker reads the phrase or sentence and repeat. Each phrase or sentence should be read as one breath group. Pay special attention to the linking of sounds between words within the breath group.

1. México y España   5. Tenemos hambre y sed.

2. un hombre y una mujer   6. Son ingleses y alemanes.

3. Escuchen y escriban.   7. Ana y yo teníamos sueño.

4. Usted y ella aprenden mucho. 8. Hay que hablar y escribir.

III. Structure drills. Listening and writing drills

A. Formal command forms

The speaker will read six sentences. Each sentence will be read twice. Write them. After you have finished, change each one to a singular and then to a plural formal command, following the model.

MODEL: Carlos trae el café.   *Carlos trae el café.*
         Carlos, traiga usted el café. Traigan ustedes el café.

1. ....

....

2. ....

....

3. ....

....

4. ....

....

5. ....

....

6. ....

....

B. Dictation

Get ready to write the sentences you will hear. Each sentence will be read twice. After the first reading, try to write all that you have heard; after the second reading, fill in what you have missed.

1. ....

2. ....

3. ....

4. ....

5. ....

NAME ....

SECTION ....

DATE ....

Lección 12

All exercises are to be done in conjunction with the tape for Lección 12, Reel 7.

I. Dialogue exercise

The speaker will ask ten questions based on the dialogue. Indicate the correct answer to each question by circling the letter before it.

1. a. dos estudiantes
   b. Jaime y Miguel
   c. los padres de Miguel Ramos

2. a. en Madrid
   b. en Córdoba
   c. en Granada

3. a. durante el siglo quince
   b. durante el siglo ocho
   c. durante los siglos diez y once

4. a. si estaban cansados
   b. si hicieron reservas
   c. si deseaban cenar

5. a. el segundo piso
   b. el tercer piso
   c. el primer piso

6. a. no cobran nada
   b. doscientas pesetas
   c. cuatrocientas pesetas

7. a. conviene registrarse
   b. conviene verlo
   c. conviene hacer reservas

8. a. que es pequeño
   b. que les gusta
   c. que les parece caro

9. a. sí, es la primera vez
   b. no, es la cuarta vez
   c. no, es la segunda vez

10. a. al primer piso
    b. al segundo piso
    c. al piso principal

II. Pronunciation drill

Review of diphthongs

The speaker will read twelve words. Each word will be read twice. Most of them will contain diphthong

sounds that you have studied. Write in the space provided the words you hear that contain a diphthong.
A few of the words will not contain a diphthong; do not include them in your list.

1. ....
2. ....
3. ....
4. ....
5. ....
6. ....
7. ....
8. ....
9. ....
10. ....
11. ....
12. ....

III. Structure drills. Listening and writing drills

A. Get ready to write, in Spanish, the four dates that the speaker will read. Each date will be read twice.

1. ....
....

2. ....
....

3. ....
....

4. ....
....

B. The speaker will read ten verb forms. Each form will be read twice. Write each one. Then, after you have finished, change singular forms to the corresponding plural forms, and plural forms to the corresponding singular ones.

1. ....
2. ....
3. ....
4. ....
5. ....
6. ....
7. ....
8. ....
9. ....
10. ....

168

Lección 13

*All exercises are to be done in conjunction with the tape
for Lección 13, Reel 7.*

I. Dialogue exercise

The speaker will read ten unfinished sentences based on the dialogue. Each unfinished sentence will be read twice. For each one, select the phrase that best completes the sentence and circle the letter before it.

1. a. Mérida
   b. Monterrey
   c. la isla de Cozumel

2. a. ir al cine
   b. ir de compras
   c. ir a la biblioteca

3. a. el mercado
   b. un buen restaurante
   c. una joyería típica

4. a. unos collares
   b. unos aretes de oro
   c. unos cinturones

5. a. el collar
   b. los aretes
   c. la pulsera

6. a. su madre
   b. Clara
   c. su hermana

7. a. unos pantalones
   b. una cartera
   c. un sombrero de paja fina

8. a. para sus hijas
   b. para Miguel
   c. para su esposa

9. a. el hotel
   b. la plaza
   c. el mercado

10. a. otros artículos para regalos
    b. unas hamacas
    c. unos anillos de plata

II. Pronunciation drill

Breath groups and word stress

Get ready to write the four sentences you will hear. Each sentence will be read twice. After you have written the sentences, divide each one into breath groups by means of a vertical line (|) and underline the first and last stressed syllables of each breath group, following the model. Note that conjunctions (**que, si**), prepositions (**de, para, por**), forms of the definite article (**el**), and object pronouns (**me, lo**) are not stressed words.

MODEL: Aquí no puedes volver si despúes quieres devolverlo.
Aquí no puedes volver | si despúes quieres devolverlo.

1. ....

2. ....

3. ....

4. ....

III. Structure drills. Listening and writing drills in the preterit indicative tense.

A. The speaker will read ten verb forms. Each form will be read twice. Write each one. After you have finished, change singular forms to the corresponding plural forms and plural forms to the corresponding singular ones.

1. ....

2. ....

3. ....

4. ....

5. ....

6. ....

7. ....

8. ....

9. ....

10. ....

B. Dictation

Get ready to write the sentences you will hear. Each sentence will be read twice. After the first reading, try to write all that you have heard; after the second reading, fill in what you have missed.

1. ....

2. ....

3. ....

4. ....

5. ....

170

Lección 14

*All exercises are to be done in conjunction with the tape
for Lección 14, Reel 8.*

I. Dialogue exercise

The speaker will read ten statements based on the dialogue. Each statement will be read twice. Circle **sí** if the statement is correct; circle **no** if it is incorrect.

1. sí   no   6. sí   no

2. sí   no   7. sí   no

3. sí   no   8. sí   no

4. sí   no   9. sí   no

5. sí   no   10. sí   no

II. Pronunciation exercise

The pronunciation of diphthongs and other vowel combinations, and linking within the breath group

The speaker will read four sentences. Each sentence will be read twice. Write each one. After you have finished, circle the diphthongs and combine by means of a linking sign (‿) the sounds between words that should be pronounced in one syllable, following the model.

MODEL: Juan estaba aquí.   *Juan estaba aquí.*   J (ua) n‿estaba‿aquí.

1. ....

2. ....

3. ....

4. ....

III. Structure drills. Listening and writing drills

A. The speaker will read ten verb forms. Each form will be read twice. Write each one. After you have finished, change singular forms to the corresponding plural forms, and plural forms to the corresponding singular ones.

1. ....

2. ....

3. ....

4. ....

5. ....

6. ....

7. ....

8. ....

9. ....

10. ....

B. You will hear five sentences in English. Each sentence will be read twice. Write them. After you have finished, write the Spanish equivalent of each one.

1. ....

....

2. ....

....

3. ....

....

4. ....

....

5. ....

....

Lección 15

All exercises are to be done in conjunction with the tape for Lección 15, Reel 8.

I. Dialogue exercise

The speaker will ask ten questions based on the dialogue. For each one, select the phrase that best answers the queston and circle the letter before it.

1. a. en la playa

   b. en su apartamento

   c. en la isla de Cozumel

2. a. al padre de Alberto

   b. a Luis Śanchez

   c. a varios amigos

3. a. no, es un profesor inglés

   b. sí, es un estudiante hispanoamericano

   c. no, es un estudiane inglés

4. a. el libro de español

   b. una revista mexicana

   c. la sección de deportes

5. a. unos bailes fantásticos

   b. la final de la Copa Mundial

   c. un partido de béisbol

6. a. a la una de la tarde

   b. a las dos de la tarde

   c. a las once de la mañana

7. a. -¿A quién busca usted?

   b. -Te esperábamos ayer.

   c. -!Hola, Luis, pasa!

8. a. el desayuno

   b. el almuerzo

   c. maníes y unas bebidas

9. a. un hermano de Jorge

   b. Luis

   c. Jorge

10. a. para ir de compras

    b. para hacer una cita con él

    c. para cenar con él

II. Intonation drill

Intonation pattern of a declarative sentence that consists of one breath group

When you hear the number, read the corresponding sentence aloud as one breath group, applying the principles you have just heard. Then listen as the speaker reads the sentence and repeat.

1. Los jóvenes esperan a Luis Sánchez.

2. Hay mucha gente en las canchas.

3. Nos alegramos mucho de verte.

4. Tú deberías jugar más al tenis.

5. Ya salen los dos equipos.

III. Structure drills. Listening and writing drills

A. The speaker will read ten verb forms. Each form will be read twice. Write each one. Then change the forms in the future tense to the corresponding conditional forms, and the forms in the conditional tense to the corresponding future indicative forms.

1. ....

2. ....

3. ....

4. ....

5. ....

6. ....

7. ....

8. ....

9. ....

10. ....

B. You will hear five sentences in English. Each sentence will be read twice. Write them. After you have finished, write the Spanish equivalent of each one.

1. ....

....

2. ....

....

3. ....

....

4. ....

....

5. ....

....

174

Lección 16

All exercises are to be done in conjunction with the tape for Lección 16, Reel 9.

I. Dialogue exercise

The speaker will read ten unfinished sentences based on the dialogue. Each unfinished sentence will be read twice. For each one, select the phrase that best completes the sentence and circle the letter before it.

1. a. en su apartamento
   b. en el hospital
   c. en su oficina

2. a. unos libros
   b. unas flores
   c. unos regalos

3. a. estaba en la peluquería
   b. estaba enferma
   c. estaba en el centro

4. a. el brazo
   b. la cabeza
   c. todo el cuerpo

5. a. como la semana pasada
   b. como hace unos días
   c. como ayer

6. a. le dolían las piernas
   b. tosió muchísimo
   c. tenía mucha fiebre

7. a. unas revistas españolas
   b. unas toallas
   c. un jarabe para la tos

8. a. tantas píldoras
   b. tantas aspirinas
   c. tantas medicinas

9. a. volver a casa pronto
   b. hacerle caso al médico
   c. descansar unos días

10. a. arquitectura
    b. derecho
    c. medicina

II. Intonation drill

Intonation pattern of a declarative sentence of two or more breath groups

When you hear the number, read the corresponding sentence aloud, dividing it into two breath groups and applying the principles you have just heard. Then listen as the speaker reads the sentence and repeat.

1. Al salir de la iglesia, visitaron a su amiga.

2. Pasamos por la residencia y nos dijeron que estabas enferma.

3. Tengo un resfriado terrible y muchísima fiebre.

4. Espero ponerme bien lo más pronto posible.

III. Structure drills. Listening and writing drills

A. The speaker will read ten sentences. Each sentence will be read twice. Write each one. When you have finished, change each sentence first to an affirmative familiar singular command and then to a negative familiar singular command.

1. ....

....

2. ....

....

3. ....

....

4. ....

....

5. ....

....

6. ....

....

7. ....

....

8. ....

....

9. ....

....

10. ....

....

B. You will hear five sentences in English. Each sentence will be read twice. Write them. After you have finished, write the Spanish equivalent of each one.

1. ....

....

2. ....

....

3. ....

....

4. ....

....

5. ....

....

Lección 17

All exercises are to be done in conjunction with the tape for Lección 17, Reel 9.

I. Dialogue exercise

The speaker will read ten statements based on the dialogue. Each statement will be read twice. Circle **sí** if the statement is correct; circle **no** if it is incorrect.

1. sí   no   6. sí   no

2. sí   no   7. sí   no

3. sí   no   8. sí   no

4. sí   no   9. sí   no

5. sí   no   10. sí   no

II. Intonation drill

Intonation pattern of *yes | no* questions

When you hear the number, read the corresponding question aloud, applying the principles you have just heard. Then listen as the speaker reads the question and repeat.

1. ¿Quieres que comamos algo?

2. ¿Viste el apartamento?

3. ¿Tienes muchas ganas de verlo?

4. ¿Lo pongo en la lista?

5. ¿Hiciste una cita con el gerente?

III. Structure drills. Listening and writing drills

A. You will hear six incomplete sentences. Each incomplete sentence will be read twice. Write them. Then, for each one, complete the sentence with the appropriate form of the verb used in the infinitive in the first part of the sentence, as in the model.

MODEL: Ana quiere ir, pero yo prefiero que tú ....
Ana quiere ir, pero yo prefiero que tú vayas.

1. ....

....

2. ....

....

3. ....

....

4. ....

....

5. ....

....

6. ....

....

B. Dictation

Get ready to write the sentences you will hear. Each sentence will be read twice. After the first reading, try to write all that you have heard; after the second reading, fill in what you have missed.

1. ....

....

2. ....

....

3. ....

4. ....

5. ....

Lección 18

All exercises are to be done in conjunction with the tape for Lección 18, Reel 10.

I. Dialogue exercise

The speaker will ask ten questions based on the dialogue. For each one, select the phrase that best answers the question and circle the letter before it.

1. a. el profesor de francés

   b. el profesor de economía

   c. un economista famoso

2. a. en una residencia

   b. en la biblioteca

   c. en una ciudad cercana

3. a. Alberto y Silvia

   b. Rita y Jaime

   c. cuatro compañeros

4. a. que se oigan sirenas

   b. que haya tanto tráfico

   c. que no haya tráfico

5. a. que no pueda seguir adelante

   b. que haya habido un accidente

   c. que no venga la policía

6. a. a moderar la marcha

   b. a llamar una ambulancia

   c. a organizer el tráfico

7. a. llegar al lugar del accidente

   b. seguir adelante

   c. llamar a la policía

8. a. que le permita manejar

   b. que deje que el taxista siga adelante

   c. que pase a un taxista

9. a. una ambulancia

   b. un coche patrulla

   c. un conductor mejor que Juan

10. a. que tal vez no lleguen a tiempo

    b. que quizás empiece tarde

    c. que tal vez no se dé

II. Intonation exercise

Intonation pattern of a question that starts with an interrogative word

When you hear the number, read the corresponding question aloud, applying the principles you have just heard. Then listen as the speaker reads the question and repeat.

1. ¿Cómo están ustedes?

2. ¿Cuántos libros compraste?

3. ¿Qué lista ha preparado Silvia?

4. ¿Qué le rogará a su madre?

5. ¿Cuándo buscarán apartamento?

III. Structure drills. Listening and writing drills

A. The speaker will read ten verb forms in different tenses. Each form will be read twice. Write each one. When you have finished, change each form to the corresponding present perfect subjunctive form, as in the model.

MODEL: yo digo   *yo digo*   *yo haya dicho*

1. ....

2. ....

3. ....

4. ....

5. ....

6. ....

7. ....

8. ....

9. ....

10. ....

B. The speaker will read ten unfinished sentences. Each unfinished sentence will be read twice. For each one, select the phrase that best completes the sentence and circle the letter before it.

1. a. hacen el viaje

   b. hagan el viaje

   c. harán el viaje

2. a. es español

   b. sea español

   c. ser español

3. a. lo sepa

   b. lo sabe

   c. saberlo

4. a. vendrán pronto

   b. vengan pronto

   c. venir pronto

5. a. llegará a tiempo

   b. llega a tiempo

   c. llegue a tiempo

6. a. se queden aquí

   b. se queden aquí

   c. quedarse aquí

7. a. estar enferma

   b. esté enferma

   c. está enferma

8. a. lo ha visto

   b. lo haya visto

   c. lo vio

9. a. tengamos mala suerte?

   b. tenemos mala suerte?

   c. tendremos mala suerte?

10. a. puedes venir

    b. puedas venir

    c. podrás venir

Lección 19

All exercises are to be done in conjunction with the tape for Lección 19, Reel 10.

I. Dialogue exercise

The speaker will read ten unfinished sentences based on the dialogue. Each unfinished sentence will be read twice. For each one, select the phrase that best completes the sentence and circle the letter before it.

1. a. la Facultad de Derecho

   b. una empresa norteamericana

   c. la Escuela de Ingeniería Agrícola

2. a. de un amigo mexicano

   b. del señor Ruiz

   c. de Miguel Ramos

3. a. en Suramérica

   b. en Puerto Rico

   c. en Los Ángeles

4. a. gerente de la empresa

   b. ingeniero en Puerto Rico

   c. agente de la compañía

5. a. un estudiante chileno

   b. un estudiante cubano

   c. Miguel Ramos

6. a. sepa manejar

   b. entienda de maquinaria agrícola

   c. tenga varios años de experiencia

7. a. este verano

   b. este trimestre

   c. el año que viene

8. a. casarse

   b. estudiar en México

   c. conocer la isla de Puerto Rico

9. a. pidiéndole más informes

   b. recomendando a Miguel

   c. recomendando a una señorita

10. a. no hable con nadie del puesto

    b. le escriba al señor Ruiz

    c. le traduzca unos versos

II. Intonation exercise

Intonation pattern of an exclamatory sentence

When you hear the number, read the corresponding exclamatory sentence aloud, applying the principles you have just heard. Then listen as the speaker reads the sentence and repeat.

1. ¡Cuánto se lo agradezco!

2. ¡Qué muchacha más bonita!

3. ¡Que sorpresa tan agradable!

4. ¡Qué gusto estar aquí, mamá!

5. ¡Demasiados chóferes, amigos!

III. Structure drills. Listening and writing drills

A. The speaker will read eight unfinished sentences. Each unfinished sentence will be read twice. For each one, select the phrase that best completes the sentence and circle the letter before it.

1. a. haga eso

   b. hace eso

   c. hacer eso

2. a. estudiar más

   b. estudie más

   c. estudia más

3. a. obtenga trabajo

   b. obtener trabajo

   c. obtiene trabajo

4. a. lo recomienda

   b. lo recomendará

   c. lo recomiende

5. a. lo haya visto?

   b. lo ha visto?

   c. lo verá?

6. a. ha vivido allí

   b. vivió allí

   c. haya vivido allí

7. a. está enfermo?

   b. esté enfermo?

   c. estará enfermo?

8. a. no venga

   b. no viene

   c. no vendrá

B. The speaker will read eight unfinished sentences. Each unfinished sentence will be read twice. For each one, select the phrase that best completes the sentence and circle the letter before it.

1. a. juega al fútbol

   b. juegue al fútbol

2. a. sea ingeniero

   b. es ingeniero

3. a. habla francés

   b. hable francés

4. a. es joven

   b. sea joven

5. a. sepa manejar?

   b. sabe manejar?

6. a. me ayudará

   b. me ayude

7. a. es trabajador?

   b. sea trabajador?

8. a. entiende de negocios

   b. entienda de negocios

All exercises are to be done in conjunction with the tape for Lección 20, Reel 11.

I. Dialogue exercise

The speaker will read ten statements based on the dialogue. Each statement will be read twice. Circle **sí** if the statement is correct; circle **no** if it is incorrect.

1. sí   no   6. sí   no

2. sí   no   7. sí   no

3. sí   no   8. sí   no

4. sí   no   9. sí   no

5. sí   no   10. sí   no

II. Intonation exercise

Intonation pattern of commands and requests

When you hear the number, read the corresponding command aloud, applying the principles you have just heard. Then listen as the speaker reads the command and repeat.

1. ¡Envíele usted el boleto!

2. ¡No le digas eso!

3. ¡Vámonos pronto!

4. ¡Cálmense todos!

5. ¡Que se lleven las suyas!

III. Structure drills. Listening and writing drills

A. The speaker will read ten verb forms. Each form will be read twice. Write each one. When you have finished writing all the forms, change singular forms to the corresponding plural forms, and plural forms to the corresponding singular ones.

1. ....

2. ....

3. ....

4. ....

5. ....

6. ....

7. ....

8. ....

9. ....

10. ....

B. The speaker will read ten unfinished sentences. Each unfinished sentence will be read twice. For each one, select the phrase or verb form that best completes the sentence and circle the letter before it.

1. a. las mirará

   b. las mire

   c. las mira

2. a. vuelven

   b. vuelvan

   c. volverán

3. a. la veo

   b. la veré

   c. la vea

4. a. la veo

   b. la vea

   c. la veré

5. a. suena el timbre

   b. sonó el timbre

   c. suene el timbre

6. a. comenzarán las clases

   b. comienzan las clases

   c. comiencen las clases

7. a. cancela

   b. cancelará

   c. cancele

8. a. oiremos

   b. oímos

   c. oigamos

9. a. nos lo digan

   b. decírnoslo

   c. diciéndonoslo

10. a. me lo pide

    b. me lo pida

    c. me lo pedirá

Lección 21

All exercises are to be done in conjunction with the tape for Lección 21, Reel 11.

I. Dialogue exercise

The speaker will ask ten questions based on the dialogue. For each one, select the phrase that best answers the question and circle the letter before it.

1. a. Jaime y Miguel

   b. Rita y Jaime

   c. Alberto y Silvia

2. a. sí, una vez

   b. sí, varias veces

   c. no, nunca

3. a. buscar apartamento

   b. ir al teatro

   c. llamar a José

4. a. unas maletas

   b. un mapa de Suramérica

   c. algunos consejos

5. a. un suéter

   b. un abrigo ligero

   c. un impermeable

6. a. porque llueve allí mucho

   b. porque llueve allí a veces

   c. porque no tienen un paraguas

7. a. el padre de Silvia

   b. el padre de Alberto

   c. José Soto

8. a. algunos libros

   b. algunos objetos de cerámica

   c. algunas transparencias

9. a. almorzar en el centro

   b. levantarse temprano

   c. escoger una cámara

10. a. a las nueve de la mañana

    b. a las dos de la tarde

    c. a las once en punto

II. Intonation exercise

Intonation pattern to express special interest or courtesy

Listen carefully to the following interrogative, exclamatory, and declarative sentences as they are read by the speaker. Then repeat them, imitating exactly the intonation of the speaker. Each sentence will be read twice.

1. ¿Cómo está tu hermano?

2. ¡Qué muchacha más bonita!

3. Es con Silvia con quien se casa.

4. ¡No le digas eso!

5. ¿Por qué se habrá puesto roja?

III. Structure drills. Listening and writing drills

A. The speaker will read eight unfinished sentences. Each unfinished sentence will be read twice. For each one, select the phrase or verb form that best completes the sentence and circle the letter before it.

1. a. llamaron antes

   b. llamaran antes

   c. llamarían antes

2. a. daría

   b. dará

   c. dé

3. a. dará

   b. daría

   c. daba

4. a. habrá venido en seguida

   b. vendría en seguida

   c. habría venido en seguida

5. a. se quedará con nosotros

   b. se quedaría con nosotros

   c. se queda con nosotros

6. a. si viajas por los Andes?

   b. si viajaras por los Andes?

   c. si viajabas por los Andes?

7. a. se marche

   b. se marcharía

   c. se marchara

8. a. lleváramos impermeables

   b. llevemos impermeables

   c. llevar impermeables

B. Dictation

Get ready to write the sentences you will hear. Each sentence will be read twice. After the first reading, try to write all that you have heard; after the second reading, fill in what you have missed.

1. ....

   ....

2. ....

   ....

192

3. ....

....

4. ....

5. ....

Lección 22

All exercises are to be done in conjunction with the tape for Lección 22, Reel 12.

I. Dialogue exercise

The speaker will read ten unfinished sentences based on the dialogue. Each unfinished sentence will be read twice. For each one, select the phrase that best completes the sentence and circle the letter before it.

1. a. una cafetería

   b. un hotel

   c. un restaurante

2. a. de sus viajes

   b. de sus planes

   c. de sus estudios

3. a. cubano

   b. español

   c. puertorriqueño

4. a. España

   b. Suramérica

   c. Puerto Rico

5. a. en el campo

   b. en la costa

   c. con sus abuelos

6. a. hace muchos años

   b. hace un par de años

   c. el año pasado

7. a. de economía

   b. de arquitectura

   c. de derecho

8. a. se hiciera ingeniero

   b. continuara sus estudios

   c. volviera a casa

9. a. le escribieran a menudo

   b. lo visitaran en Madrid

   c. viajaran por España

10. a. muchos recuerdos

    b. una carta

    c. un pastel

II. Intonation exercise

Review of intonation patterns

When you hear the number, read the corresponding sentence aloud, applying the principles of Spanish intonation that we have studied. Then listen as the speaker reads the sentence and repeat, imitating the intonation exactly.

1. Hay que felicitarlo.

2. Después de una deliciosa comida, charlan de sus planes.

3. ¿Qué piensas hacer tú?

4. ¿No es hora de hablar de nuestros planes?

5. ¡Tú siempre echando piropos!

III. Structure drills. Listening and writing drills

A. The speaker will read five affirmative familiar singular commands. Each command will be read twice. Write them. After you have finished, change each one to the familiar plural command form. The speaker will verify the response.

1. ....

2. ....

3. ....

4. ....

5. ....

B. The speaker will read five affirmative familiar plural commands. Each command will be read twice. Write them. After you have finished, change each one to the negative familiar plural command form. The speaker will verify the response.

1. ....

2. ....

3. ....

4. ....

5. ....

C. You will hear five sentences in English. Each sentence will be read twice. Write them. After you have finished, write the Spanish equivalent of each sentence.

1. ....

....

2. ....

....

3. ....

....

4. ....

....

5. ....

....

3 4 5 6 7 8 9 0